Fowl and Game Bird Cookery

JAMES BEARD'S
FOWL & GAME BIRD
COOKERY

Designed and illustrated by John Alcorn

AN ORIGINAL HARVEST/HBJ BOOK
HARCOURT BRACE JOVANOVICH
NEW YORK AND LONDON

Requests for permission to make copies of
any part of the work should be mailed to:
Permissions, Harcourt Brace Jovanovich, Inc.
757 Third Avenue, New York, N.Y. 10017

Printed in the United States of America

This book incorporates material
from *Fowl and Game Cookery*,
published by M. Barrows & Co., Inc., 1944.

The recipe Virginia Fried Chicken with Browned
Gravy is from *The Taste of Country Cooking*, by
Edna Lewis, copyright © 1976 by Edna Lewis,
reprinted by permission of Alfred A. Knopf, Inc.

Library of Congress Cataloging in Publication Data

Beard, James Andrews, 1903–
James Beard's Fowl and game bird cookery.

(An Original Harvest/HBJ book)
Includes index.
1. Cookery (Poultry)   2.   Cookery (Game)   I.   Title.
II.   Title: Fowl and game bird cookery.
TX750.B42   641.6'6'5   78-71061
ISBN 0-15-633340-6

FIRST ORIGINAL HARVEST/HBJ EDITION

ABCDEFGHIJ

Contents

Introduction

When the original version of this book was first published in the 1940s, the marketing of poultry was considerably different than it is today. Chicken was still in the luxury class. One shopped around for the chubbiest birds, those that had the fullest breasts and were the most likely candidates for a good meal. Still, it was a chancy affair. Broilers were sometimes long, scrawny things that had very little meat, and roasters could be equally undernourished. However, one could get very good fowl (or "mature hens," as they were sometimes called), which made a wonderful *poule au pot* or excellent broth. And wonder of wonders, one also got hens that had lovely strings of eggs in them—unborn eggs, as it were—that were a delicacy for the sauce.

Nowadays, chickens have become almost uniform. They are raised in enormous plants, and some are not even allowed to touch ground during their short lifetime. Often they are given scientific feeding, whereas in earlier times they were allowed to roam at will and eat more or less what the family ate. They brought to the table flavors of good feeding and healthy developing. However, I think there are few of us who would exchange the present availability of chickens of all types for the doubtful shopping around that we used to do.

A friend and student of mine is the head of a chicken-producing plant in California that processes close to 400,000 chickens a day. These chickens are not raised on wire but are allowed to do some running. They are scientifically fed; consultants are on duty at all times to be certain that their food is balanced to promote growth, tenderness, and reproduction. There is practically no waste in these chickens: the feet are cleaned, frozen, and shipped to China, as the Chinese use chicken feet a great deal in their cuisine; and even the feathers are processed into a powder.

I have also toured chicken compounds in Oregon, where I get extremely good chickens that are fresh, flavorful, and extraordinarily clean. Cleanliness is one of the rules of the chicken industry—a situation that is markedly different from former days. I can remember the ordeal one faced before presenting a chicken at table: drawing it (being careful not to rupture the gall sack), washing off the waste materials that may have collected on the carcass, and singeing off the little hairs and pin feathers. I don't think any modern, up-to-date cook, or at least very few, knows how to draw a chicken any longer. All this is performed for us; and the neck and giblets are removed, washed, and put into a separate package, tucked into the cavity of the chicken. It is significant to note, too, that nowadays chickens are bred and cared for so well that they require less time to cook.

Some people argue that there is no flavor left in a scientifically bred chicken, but I think that one finds a great variation in quality, from fair to excellent. I have been especially interested in the television commercials of Mr. Perdue of the Perdue Farms on the Atlantic seaboard, whose statements about his birds are honest and straightforward. He is, I must say, an effective salesman for his own product, which has a fine reputation in the Eastern market.

One interesting development in the marketing of chicken is the fact that we now have not only the whole birds, but individual parts. One can find legs and thighs, breasts, backs and necks, gizzards and hearts—all sold separately, which is a great convenience. Since I am a dark-meat man, I am far more apt to buy legs and thighs for a dish than I am to buy a whole chicken and cut it up. Likewise, the incredible number of people who specialize in serving chicken breast variations have a field day, for they can get them in abundance, either with bone or boned. In fancier markets the breast meat even comes filleted, much like veal. (One must remember that a chicken breast per se consists of two half breasts joined together by the breast bone. So if you are reading a recipe that calls for 8 chicken breasts, it is likely to mean 4 chicken breasts cut in half.)

Another advantage of chicken parts is that one can use the backs, necks, and gizzards for stock and broth. The gizzards add such a gelatinous quality, as do the bones and necks. It is a very simple and wise practice to keep stock in the freezer at all times, and to use the gizzards for other dishes as well.

The only chicken product that is difficult to find these days— probably due to the way chickens are raised—is a hen or fowl, for poaching. I was mistakenly led to something called a "roasting fowl" one day that proved to be impregnable to cooking. It didn't even make good broth. Otherwise, one can generally trust the classifications that are given for chickens of all shapes, sizes, and qualities.

The raising and marketing of turkey has changed greatly in recent times also. For the most part, we now have turkeys that are much more compact, that are raised for a full, plump breast, a problem for those of us who love the dark meat. This used to be in short supply to begin with and is even more so now.

As with chickens, turkey in parts has become a most advantageous and intelligent way to buy turkeys when one is not going to have a large, roasted bird to grace the table. And speaking of that, it is apparent by now that turkey has evolved from being the sainted holiday bird for Thanksgiving, Christmas, and New Year's to an economical family dish used the year round and in many different ways. A turkey breast can be used for a hot meal and then for various cold dishes such as turkey tonnato or turkey salad. It can also be cut into scallops and used as one would use veal scallops. One breast will carry a family through several meals. The legs and thighs can be roasted, braised, and poached; or boned, stuffed, rolled, and cooked as a type of galantine or ballotine. Turkey wings, braised, sautéed, or curried, are delicious, especially for those who like to pick bones.

Turkeys are now available frozen with extra fat inserted into their breasts to create what is called "self-basting"; some have been injected with butter, others with vegetable oil. This presumably makes them more tender and flavorful. Fresh-killed birds are obtainable in most good butcher shops, and the sizes vary tremendously. Time was when only larger birds, from 12 to 20 pounds, were sold. Now it is possible to find smaller birds of 5 or 6 pounds to 9 pounds.

There are still wild turkeys to be hunted, too, and domestic wild turkeys can be found on some farms. If you are curious, you might buy one someday and compare its bone structure with that of the full-breasted birds that we have now. It is rather surprising to see what the ancestor of our holiday turkey looks like. As for flavor, I find it a far more delicious fowl.

Ducks are found in most parts of this country, and a large portion are sold frozen, cleaned, and processed as Long Island ducklings. They have an extremely heavy layer of fat on them and have to be cooked accordingly. One can occasionally find fresh-killed, meatier ducks. And in Pennsylvania, Muscovy duck, a much leaner bird than the Long Island, is commonplace in country markets during certain seasons. In San Francisco's Chinatown, and possibly in other Chinese communities, ducks are specially processed for what is called the "Buddhist trade." They are sold complete with head and feet and are perhaps the most perfectly cleaned birds I have ever seen. (They come from farms in Petaluma, which is not far from San Francisco.) If you live in a city with a large Chinese population, you will be well repaid for making a trip to one of their markets.

The raising and distribution of smaller birds has in general kept up with the industry with the exception of squabs, which are available in fewer places than they used to be. When I was young I remember squabs in many city markets—especially in San Francisco and New York—extremely reasonable and always available. On the other hand, a bird called the "Rock Cornish game hen" or "game bird" has inundated our markets. For the most part, these small birds—a cross between a game cock and a Plymouth Rock hen—are sold processed and frozen, in which form I cannot recommend them. However, in the greater New York metropolitan area, where Frank Perdue has made them readily available, one can buy fresh Cornish game hens that are remarkably delicious. They lend themselves admirably to most ways of preparing chicken; they brown nicely, are excellent stuffed and roasted at high temperature, and are extremely good sautéed very quickly.

There has been so much change and development in the poultry industry that it might well be the most efficient of all the food suppliers in the country from the standpoint of availability, quality control, and general excellence. In addition there are game farms in operation that produce fine quail, partridge, and pheasants—both baby pheasants and fully grown ones, which are sold fresh or frozen. The pheasants are produced primarily for the restaurant trade, which uses vast numbers of them for dinners and for catering. However, they are also available to the general public and provide a festive change from the usual poultry menu. Buy them fresh, if you can, and allow them to hang in a cool place or to mature in the refrigerator for a few days before you use them. They will have a much better flavor.

While the outlook for poultry and domesticated game birds has greatly improved, some birds from the wild are less plentiful than they once were; and for most Americans, grouse is no longer to be had at all. When the earlier version of this book was written, grouse was still being flown over in season from Europe for specialty food shops and certain restaurants. Government regulations now prohibit this. So unless you have a private source, you will have to migrate to England for part of the year, if you fancy this champion of all game birds.

1

Chicken

CHICKEN CLASSIFICATIONS

SQUAB CHICKEN
The youngest of chickens on the market, weighing about a pound, and usually broiled, either split or whole. You will need one per serving. Expensive and hard to find.

CORNISH GAME HEN
Young hens, weighing 1 to 1¾ pounds (450–800 g). You will need one per serving of the smaller birds. Available fresh only in the greater metropolitan New York area. Use for roasting, sautéing or broiling.

BROILERS
These are young birds, weighing 1½ to 2½ pounds (675–1125 g), and extremely tender. They should be firmly meated, with a little fat on them. Use for broiling and some sautéing. Sometimes cooked whole, they are generally split in half. In this case, remove the back and neck with poultry shears and press down firmly to flatten the two halves and allow more even cooking. One-half broiler is considered a portion.

FRYERS OR BROILER-FRYERS
These all-purpose birds weigh between 2 and 3½ pounds (900–1500 g). They are cooked either split, as is the case with broilers, or cut into smaller serving portions and broiled, sautéed, fried, or braised. Be sure to cut—do not chop—the chicken. Slice be-

3

tween the legs and body through the thigh joint. Cut each leg and thigh in half at the joint. Then cut through the wing joints. Next split the carcass, using poultry shears. The breast can be boned out or left intact and cut into two pieces; or, in the case of a large and meaty chicken, cut into three pieces. Cut the back and rib cage into two or three pieces. (Always include these for people who love to pick bones. I am one.) Thus, you can get as many as twelve pieces from one bird.

ROASTERS
Larger birds ranging from 4 to 6 pounds (1¾–2¾ kg). They may be used for poaching as well as roasting.

CAPONS
Capons are unsexed male birds whose flesh is tender and delicate. These weigh up to 8 or 9 pounds (3½–4 kg) and should be considered if you are serving more than four people. They are no longer hormone fed, due to government regulations, so you should feel quite safe in using them. More expensive than other chickens.

FOWL
A mature or old hen, used for poaching or for fricassees, and wonderful eating if you can find one. Ranging in weight from 4 to 8 pounds (1¾–3½ kg), they are usually well-retired layers. However, they are seldom found in markets nowadays, and the fowl that does appear is, in my opinion, only worthy of being used to make strong broth. Beware of something called a "roasting fowl"; it will never tenderize by roasting.

SAUTÉED CHICKEN

Chicken is sautéed as often as it is fried, although people tend to confuse the two terms. The difference lies in the amount of fat used. A small amount is used for sautéing; in frying, the food is well steeped in fat or entirely covered with it.

Buy broilers or small fryers for a sauté. Tiny chickens can be sautéed whole. Larger chickens should be cut in half or in convenient serving pieces. And be sure the giblets are included, for they make a sauté even better.

The prime utensil to use for this form of cookery is an iron skillet or sauté pan, although any heavy pan—cast aluminum, stainless steel, or enamel on iron—can be used. The pan should be equipped with a lid that fits tightly.

Any choice of fats can be used. Clarified butter is the finest, followed by olive oil, peanut oil, and corn oil; margarine gives acceptable results, too; and bacon fat is wonderful, although it brings another flavor into your dish.

To sauté, heat a light film of butter or other fat in the pan. Depending on the amount of chicken being prepared, you will generally need 2 to 5 tablespoons. Brown the chicken on all sides over a brisk flame, then cover and let tenderize over low heat. If you are making a sauce for the dish, remove the pieces of chicken to a hot platter while you prepare it. To rewarm, either return the chicken to the pan and heat with the sauce for a few moments, or keep the chicken warm on a hot platter and pour the sauce over it.

Basic Chicken Sauté

2 broilers or fryers, 2
    pounds (900 g) each
6 tablespoons (85 g) butter
Flour for dredging (op-
    tional)
Salt and freshly ground
    black pepper

½ cup (1 dL) dry white
    wine
3 to 4 tablespoons chopped
    parsley

Each chicken should be cut into four pieces—two breast halves with the wings attached, and the two legs and thighs with part of the backbone. Wipe the chicken with a damp cloth if you wish.

Sautés should not be overcrowded in the pan. Therefore, since you are preparing two chickens, it might be wise to use two pans, putting the white meat in one and the dark meat in the other, since they require different cooking times.

Melt the butter in one very large heavy skillet or two smaller ones with a tight-fitting lid or lids. Add the chicken pieces and

brown them over medium-high heat on all sides. (For a deeper
color, flour the chicken first). Season to taste with salt and pepper, then reduce the heat, cover, and cook very gently for about
5 to 8 minutes. Remove the cover or covers and rearrange the
pieces so they will cook evenly. Add ¼ cup (½ dL) wine, re-
cover, and cook 10 minutes more. Uncover and move the pieces
of white meat to the top (if using one skillet), leaving the dark
meat, which takes longer to cook, on the bottom. Cover and
cook until the chicken is just tender and done, but still juicy,
about 5 to 10 minutes more.

Remove the chicken pieces to a hot platter. Add the remaining wine and the parsley to the pan or pans, turn up the heat, and
boil, scraping up the brown glaze from the bottom with a wooden
spoon. When the juices have reduced a little, pour over the
chicken.

Serves four.

A Sauté with White Wine and Herbs I

2 broilers or fryers, 2
pounds (900 g) each,
quartered
6 tablespoons (85 g) butter
1 medium onion, finely
chopped
Salt and freshly ground
black pepper

1 tablespoon each chopped
fresh parsley, chives,
chervil, and tarragon
(or substitute 1 tea-
spoon dried herbs
where necessary)
½ cup (1 dL) dry white
wine
Lemon juice to taste

Brown the chicken pieces in the butter in one very large skillet
or two smaller ones. Add the finely chopped onion, reduce the
heat, and cover. Cook for about 10 minutes. Rearrange the
pieces to cook evenly, and cook until tender, about 10 minutes
more. Season to taste with salt and pepper, and add the herbs.
Pour the wine over the chicken, cover, and let it cook down
with the herbs, onion, and chicken juices. Degrease the sauce and
correct the seasoning. Just before serving, add a few drops of
freshly squeezed lemon juice. This is delicious with crusty fried
potatoes and puréed spinach.

Serves four.

A Sauté with White Wine and Herbs II

1 broiler, 2 pounds (900 g),
   split
¼ cup (½ dL) olive oil
½ cup (1 dL) white wine
Salt and freshly ground
   black pepper

1 tablespoon each chopped
   fresh parsley, basil,
   summer savory, and
   mint (or substitute 1
   teaspoon dried herbs
   where necessary)
Pinch of thyme
1½ teaspoons (8 g) butter

Heat the oil in a skillet and brown the chicken quickly over high heat. Reduce the heat and continue cooking for 12 minutes. Add the white wine, salt and pepper to taste, and the herbs. Turn the chicken well so that it becomes coated with the herbs. Cover and simmer till tender. Transfer the chicken to a warm platter. At the last minute add the butter to the pan juices, and pour over the chicken. Serve with grilled tomatoes and a green salad.

   Serves two.

A Sauté with Tomato

2 broilers or fryers, 2
   pounds each (900 g),
   quartered
6 tablespoons (85 g) butter
Flour for dredging (op-
   tional)
Salt and freshly ground
   black pepper
3 tablespoons finely
   chopped onion

1 small clove garlic, finely
   chopped
½ cup (1 dL) dry white
   wine
3 medium tomatoes, peeled,
   seeded, and chopped
1 tablespoon chopped
   parsley

Brown the chicken pieces as directed under Basic Chicken Sauté (page 5) and season. Reduce the heat and add the onion and garlic. Cover and cook for 5 minutes. Add the wine, cover, and cook for 10 minutes. Add the tomatoes, cover, and cook 10 minutes more. Remove the chicken to a hot platter. Add parsley to the sauce and let it cook down for a minute or so. Correct the seasoning and pour over the chicken.

   Serves four.

Jeanne Owen's Sauté with Tarragon

2 broilers, 2 pounds (900 g)
 each, quartered
1 tablespoon dried or 2
 tablespoons fresh
 tarragon

1 cup (¼ L) Riesling wine
8 tablespoons (115 g)
 butter
Salt and freshly ground
 black pepper

Prepare the broilers for sauté. Soak the tarragon in ½ cup (1 dL) Riesling for 30 minutes. Melt the butter in one very large heavy skillet or two smaller ones and brown the pieces of chicken quickly. Add the remaining Riesling and reduce the heat. Add salt and pepper to taste. Cover and cook for 15 minutes. About 5 minutes before the chicken is done, add the soaked tarragon. Turn the chicken in this several times, then cook 5 to 10 minutes more, or until tender. Arrange on a hot platter. Swirl the pan juices over high heat for 2 minutes and pour over the chicken.
 Serves four.

A Lemon Sauté

9 tablespoons (130 g)
 butter
1 broiler-fryer, 3½ pounds
 (1500 g), quartered
Salt and freshly ground
 black pepper

Juice of 2 lemons
Finely grated zest of 1
 lemon
Chopped parsley

Heat 6 tablespoons (85 g) butter in a heavy skillet and brown the chicken pieces. Season to taste, reduce the heat, and cover. Cook very gently for about 25 minutes, turning twice.
 Melt the remaining 3 tablespoons (45 g) butter in a separate pan and let it brown slightly. Just before removing the cooked chicken from the pan, pour the lemon juice and zest over it. Cook for a minute, sprinkle with chopped parsley, and remove to a hot platter. Pour over it the pan juices and browned butter.
 During asparagus season, serve this dish with cooked asparagus lightly dusted with Parmesan cheese, arranging it around the chicken on the platter. You might also serve tiny new potatoes with chopped chives, and crusty French bread.
 Serves four.

A Sauté with Mushrooms

2 broilers, 2 pounds (900 g)
    each, split
Flour for dredging
Salt and freshly ground
    black pepper
4 tablespoons (60 g)
    butter or other fat

1 tablespoon chopped onion
1 cup (60 g) tiny mushroom
    caps or sliced mush-
    rooms

Dredge the chicken halves with flour, salt, and pepper. Melt the butter or other fat in one very large skillet or two smaller ones and brown the chicken well on all sides. Reduce the heat and add the onion and the mushroom caps or sliced mushrooms. Cover the pan or pans and simmer for 10 minutes. Uncover, turn the chicken, and cook till tender. Correct the seasoning and arrange on a hot platter with the mushrooms and pan juices poured around it. Serve with fresh peas and a tossed green salad. Serves four.

A Sauté with Peppers

4 or 5 green or red sweet
    peppers
2 small broilers or 1 large
    fryer, 3½ pounds
    (1500 g) in all,
Flour for dredging
Salt and freshly ground
    black pepper
2/3 cup (1½ dL) olive oil
    or cooking oil

2 tablespoons chopped
    onion
1 clove garlic, finely
    chopped
2 large tomatoes, peeled,
    seeded, and finely
    chopped
Lemon juice to taste
1 tablespoon chopped
    parsley

Broil the green or red peppers till skins are blackened and loosened from the flesh. Remove the skins and seeds and cut into strips. Set aside.

Prepare chicken for sauté. Dredge with flour, salt, and pepper. Heat the olive oil or cooking oil in one large, heavy skillet or two smaller ones and brown the chicken, turning frequently to get an evenness of color. Reduce the heat, add the onion and garlic, cover, and cook for 10 minutes. Add the tomatoes and let

cook down for about 5 minutes, turning the chicken in the sauce several times. Add the pepper strips and heat through. Correct the seasoning, and just before serving add a few drops of lemon juice and the chopped parsley. This is excellent with polenta.
Serves four.

A Sauté with Onions

2 large Spanish onions,
  thinly sliced
7 tablespoons (100 g)
  butter
3 tablespoons vegetable oil

1 fryer, 3½ pounds
  (1500 g), cut up
Salt and freshly ground
  black pepper, to taste

Place the thinly sliced onion in a heavy-bottomed skillet over low heat and stir until it begins to color. Then add 4 tablespoons (60 g) butter and allow to brown. Meanwhile, in another large skillet, melt 3 tablespoons (45 g) butter with the oil. Brown the dark meat over fairly high heat. Add the white meat and brown, then add the browned onions. Add salt and pepper to taste. Cover the pan and simmer for 12 to 15 minutes, or until the chicken is tender. Arrange on a hot platter with the onions and serve with sautéed potatoes and a green salad.
Serves four.

A Sauté with Cabbage

2 broilers, 2 pounds (900 g)
  each, split
Flour for dredging
11 tablespoons (155 g)
  butter
Salt and freshly ground
  black pepper

1 medium head cabbage,
  shredded
1½ teaspoons caraway
  seeds
1½ cups (3½ dL) heavy
  cream

Flour the chicken. Heat 8 tablespoons (115 g) butter in one very large skillet or two smaller ones and brown the chicken. Add salt and pepper to taste and continue cooking for about 10 minutes.
Meanwhile, wash the shredded cabbage. Cook in 2 cups salted water till almost tender, about 5 minutes. Drain and toss with 3 tablespoons butter (45 g) and the caraway seeds. Add to the

chicken. Pour the cream over, cover, and let simmer for 10 minutes. Taste for seasoning and serve.

Serves four.

A Sauté with Ham

2 small broilers or 1 large fryer, 3½ pounds (1500 g) in all, cut up
8 tablespoons (115 g) butter
2 thin slices smoked ham, cut into julienne
1 medium onion, very finely chopped
1 large clove garlic, grated
1 cup (60 g) sliced mushrooms
Several sprigs of parsley, coarsely chopped
Salt and freshly ground black pepper
½ cup (1 dL) white wine

Melt the butter in one large, heavy skillet or two smaller ones. Add the chicken pieces and brown on all sides. Reduce the heat and add the smoked ham, onion, and garlic. Sauté for 10 minutes. Add the mushrooms and parsley. Turn the chicken; add salt and pepper to taste. Cover and cook another 10 to 12 minutes, or till tender. About 5 minutes before the chicken is done, add the white wine and let it cook down. Remove the chicken to a hot platter and pour the sauce over it. Serve with corn pudding or spoonbread.

Serves four.

A Sauté with Oysters

4 to 6 chicken legs with thighs
4 tablespoons (60 g) butter
1 cup (¼ L) clarified butter, or as needed
Salt and freshly ground black pepper
Flour for dredging
18 oysters, shucked and liquor reserved
2 egg yolks, beaten
1½ to 2 cups (170–225 g) cracker crumbs, or as needed
¼ cup (½ dL) sherry
Chopped parsley

Heat the 4 tablespoons of butter in a skillet and brown the chicken over a brisk flame. Add salt and pepper to taste. Cover and sauté till tender, about 15 to 20 minutes.

While the chicken is cooking, flour the oysters and dip in beaten egg yolk, then in cracker crumbs, and fry in ½ inch (1¼ cm) clarified butter till nicely browned. Season to taste. Remove the chicken and oysters from their pans and arrange on a hot platter. Add the oyster liquor to the oyster pan and heat it well, scraping the residue from the pan into the sauce. Add this, along with the sherry, to the pan in which the chicken was cooked and let it cook down for a minute or two. Pour over the chicken and oysters, sprinkle with chopped parsley, and serve.

Serves four.

A Sauté with Curry and Tomato Sauce

3 tablespoons (45 g) butter
1 broiler, 2 pounds (900 g),
    split
Salt and freshly ground
    black pepper
1 medium onion, very finely
    chopped
1 cup (¼ L) fresh tomato
    purée
2 tablespoons curry powder

Melt the butter in a heavy skillet and brown the chicken over brisk heat. Reduce the heat, add salt and pepper to taste and the onion. Cover and cook until the chicken is tender, about 20 to 25 minutes. Remove to a hot platter or casserole.

Add the tomato purée and curry powder to the pan juices and let it cook down for several minutes, stirring to create a good blend. Taste for seasoning. Pour steaming hot over the chicken, and serve with boiled rice and a little chutney.

Serves two.

A Viennese Sauté

1 chicken, 2 pounds
    (900 g), quartered
3 tablespoons (45 g)
    clarified butter or
    other fat
1 tablespoon chopped onion
2 tablespoons paprika
Salt and freshly ground
    black pepper to taste
½ cup (1 dL) heavy cream
½ cup (1 dL) chicken
    broth
1 tablespoon (15 g) butter
Dash of lemon juice
Chopped parsley

Prepare the chicken for sauté. Cook very gently in the clarified butter or other fat until delicately browned. Add the onion, paprika, and salt and pepper and cook until well blended. Reduce the heat, cover, and simmer gently for 10 minutes. Remove the chicken to a hot platter. Add to the pan the cream and the chicken broth, which can be made from the giblets. Then add 1 tablespoon butter and let the sauce reduce over brisk heat for 3 to 4 minutes. Finally add a dash of lemon juice and a sprinkling of parsley. Pour the sauce around the chicken. Serve with thin slices of zucchini sautéed in garlic and olive oil.

Serves two.

A Southwestern Sauté

This is a purely American Southwest version of the sauté, and one that has a delicious tang. I had it first at the home of a friend in Arizona. It was served with a large dish of polenta, made with water-ground cornmeal flavored with butter and grated Parmesan cheese. We washed it all down with a bottle of rough, rich claret.

2 broilers or fryers, 2
    pounds (900 g) each,
    quartered
6 to 8 thin slices of bacon
Flour for dredging
Salt and freshly ground
    black pepper to taste
2 teaspoons paprika
Sprinkle of cayenne
2 cloves garlic, finely
    chopped

1 small white onion, finely
    chopped
1 cup (¼ L) tomato purée
2 teaspoons chili powder
Sweet basil, fresh or dried,
    to taste
1/3 cup (¾ dL) dry red
    wine
Chopped parsley

Prepare chickens for sauté. Fry the bacon in a large skillet till crisp and free of most of the fat. Remove the bacon and keep warm. Dredge the chicken with flour and brown it quickly in the hot bacon fat. Add salt and pepper, the paprika, cayenne, garlic, and onion. Reduce the heat, cover, and cook for 10 minutes. Then add the tomato purée, chili powder, and sweet basil to taste. Allow this to simmer for another 10 minutes, or until the chicken is tender. Remove to a hot platter. Add the red wine to

the pan juices and cook down for 3 minutes. Taste for seasoning. Pour the sauce over the chicken, sprinkle with chopped parsley, and garnish with the bacon.
Serves six.

Chicken Breasts with Mushroom Sauce

3 whole chicken breasts, cut
   in half, skinned, and
   boned
Salt and freshly ground
   black pepper
Lemon juice to taste
Flour for dredging
2 eggs, lightly beaten
1 ½ to 2 cups (85–115 g)
   bread crumbs made
   from crustless day-old
   French bread

4 tablespoons (60 g) butter,
   more if needed
3 tablespoons olive oil
¾ pound (340 g) small,
   whole mushrooms
¼ cup (½ dL) Madeira
¾ cup (1 ¾ dL) heavy
   cream
1 egg yolk
¼ teaspoon ground allspice

Flatten the chicken breasts slightly between two sheets of waxed paper and season lightly with salt, pepper, and lemon juice. Flour the pieces, dip into the lightly beaten egg, then coat with the bread crumbs. Put on a plate and chill for 1 hour.

Heat the butter and oil in a large skillet and sauté the breasts over moderately low heat for 3 minutes on each side, or until they are just cooked through and browned. Transfer the breasts to a hot platter and keep them warm. In the same skillet sauté the mushrooms for 2 to 3 minutes, or until browned, adding more butter if necessary. Using a slotted spoon, transfer the mushrooms to a dish. Pour the fat from the skillet and add the Madeira. Reduce the liquid by half over high heat, scraping in the brown bits clinging to the bottom and sides of the pan.

In a bowl, combine the heavy cream, egg yolk, ¼ teaspoon salt, allspice, and pepper to taste. Gradually stir the cream mixture into the reduced liquid over low heat. Do not allow to boil. Add the reserved mushrooms and continue to cook the sauce over low heat, stirring until thickened. Pour the sauce over the breasts and serve with saffron rice.
Serves six.

Chicken Breasts Armagnac

2 whole chicken breasts,
halved, with wings
attached
8 tablespoons (115 g)
butter
Salt and freshly ground
black pepper

6 to 8 shallots, peeled and
chopped extremely fine
2 egg yolks
¾ cup (1¾ dL) heavy
cream
1/3 cup (¾ dL) Armagnac

Brown the chicken in the butter in a heavy skillet. Add salt and
pepper and continue to cook for about 10 to 12 minutes, turning the pieces frequently. When done, transfer to a hot platter.
    Add the shallots to the skillet and cook until tender. Reduce
heat and slowly add the egg yolks and cream, beaten together.
Cook over low heat, stirring constantly, until thoroughly blended
and thickened; do not allow to boil.
    Set the skillet aside. Heat the Armagnac and quickly pour it
over the chicken; flambé. When the Armagnac is almost burned
out, pour the sauce around the chicken. Serve with rice pilaf.
    Serves two to four.

Chicken Yucatan

2 whole chicken breasts, cut
in half, or 4 thighs and
legs
Flour for dredging
3 tablespoons (45 g) butter
3 tablespoons olive oil
Salt and freshly ground
black pepper
1/3 cup (¾ dL) Cognac
1 can (6 ounces; 1¾ dL)
undiluted, frozen con-
centrated orange juice

1 can (4 ounces; 113 g)
peeled green chilies,
drained and finely
chopped
1 clove garlic, finely
chopped
½ cup (55 g) pine nuts
¼ cup (30 g) currants or
sultana raisins
Chopped parsley

Remove the rib bones from the chicken breasts, if using, and
trim them neatly. Dust lightly with flour. Heat the butter and oil
in a skillet and lightly sear the chicken on both sides until ivory
colored. Add salt and pepper to taste. Warm the Cognac, pour

over the chicken, and flambé. Add the orange juice concentrate, chilies, and garlic. Simmer for approximately 10 minutes, or until the chicken is just tender. Turn several times during the cooking. Remove to a hot platter.

Let the sauce cook down for a minute. Pour over the chicken and sprinkle with the pine nuts, currants, and chopped parsley. Serve with rice.

Serves four.

Sautéed Chicken Wings

1 pound (450 g) chicken
    wings
4 tablespoons (60 g) butter

Salt and freshly ground
    black pepper
    to taste

Heat the butter in a heavy skillet. Add the chicken wings and sauté gently for 12 to 15 minutes, turning often. Add salt and pepper and cover the pan for about 10 minutes. Serve with new potatoes and green peas.

Serves two to three.

VARIATIONS

1. Sauté 5 or 6 bacon strips, remove, and add the wings to the bacon fat. Proceed as above. Garnish with the bacon.
2. Add 2 medium onions, finely chopped, to the sauté. When the wings are well browned, add 1 cup (¼ L) tomato sauce, 1 tablespoon chopped parsley, a pinch of dried thyme, and 3 or 4 pitted olives, cut in thin slices. Simmer, covered, for 15 minutes. Serve with rice.
3. Add 2 teaspoons paprika to the sauté. Just before serving, add ½ cup (1 dL) heavy cream and blend well.

John Beard's Sautéed Chicken

My father, who came of stalwart pioneer stock—he crossed the continent to Oregon in a covered wagon when he was five—had many definite ideas about food and life. Not only did he have the ideas, but he worked at them with a vengeance. One of them, which became a tradition in our home, must have had its influence on me at an early age.

Father felt that he could sauté a chicken better than anyone else in the family, in fact better than anyone else he had ever known. He liked a young chicken sautéed for Sunday morning breakfast. So early on Sunday—Father was never a late sleeper —he could be found in the kitchen complete with chicken, utensils, and apron. No one dared set foot in the "domestic offices" till the chicken was in the pan and wafting its glorious aroma throughout the lower floor of the house. He never would keep doors closed.

Father cut the chickens, or chicken, in ten pieces and dredged them lightly with flour. He then cut several slices of bacon from "the side" (don't think for one minute that sliced bacon was ever allowed in his house) and cut it in thin strips. These were tried out over a slow fire so that they became crisp and left a good deal of delicious fat in the iron skillet. The strips were removed to a platter, which was heating, and the pieces of chicken were lovingly lowered into the hot bacon fat. These he seared quickly, turning them and arranging them in the pan so that each morsel received the same degree of brownness and crispness.

Then the pan was covered, the flame turned low, and the chicken simmered for about 15 minutes. The cover was then removed and the pieces allowed just a few more minutes to take on additional crispness before being transferred to a hot platter.

Next came another rite: a heaping tablespoon of flour was put in the pan, after all the excess grease had been poured off, and was blended thoroughly with the little bits of goodness left in the pan. When these bits had been scraped around and melted with the flour, 2 cups of rich milk were poured in, the careful stirring began, and the seasoning was added, to Father's taste. He loved freshly ground black pepper and seemed to have a magic touch with it, for no one else I know has ever made it blend and yet retain its individuality the way Father did. When the sauce had achieved the proper degree of thickness for him, it was transferred to a hot bowl and breakfast was announced.

Of course, I neglected to say that he admitted someone else to the kitchen in time to make a huge pan of crispy hot biscuits or an iron pan filled with magnificent popovers. But I am not discussing baking in this book.

Need I add that friends of the family and of mine were always pleased to stay overnight at our house?

FRIED CHICKEN

Though its origins go back to English and Viennese cooking, fried chicken has become a distinctively American tradition, especially in the South, where it was transformed into a great Creole specialty. The ease with which it can be prepared, and the increasing abundance of chicken, has made it one of our most ubiquitous and most popular national dishes, found at drive-ins, quick-food chain restaurants, and small local restaurants from coast to coast.

Our renowned Southern-fried chicken, which is often really sautéed rather than fried, comes in many forms, variously known as chicken Maryland, Virginia fried chicken, or Creole fried chicken. Essentially a very simple dish, its success depends on the care with which it is cooked. It can be floured, breaded, or dipped in batter; and the cooking can be done in lard, lard and butter, or vegetable oil. Whatever the variation, the chicken must have a crisp golden-brown coating and a juicy interior, while absorbing a minimum of cooking fat.

Creole Fried Chicken

1 fryer, 3 to 4 pounds
    (1500–1800 g), cut
    into 8 pieces
Lemon juice
2 eggs
1/3 cup (3/4 dL) milk

Flour for dredging
Rolled cracker crumbs
Lard or cooking oil for deep
    frying
Salt and freshly ground
    black pepper

Rub the chicken well with lemon juice. Beat the eggs with the milk, coat the chicken with the mixture, and let stand for 1 to 1 1/2 hours. Then roll each piece in flour and cracker crumbs and drop into enough medium-hot lard or cooking oil to cover the chicken completely. Cook for 15 to 18 minutes or until the chicken is well browned. Season with salt and pepper to taste and drain on paper towels.

Serves four.

Chicken Maryland

There are countless recipes for this dish, and which is the original I cannot tell you. Escoffier, in his book *Ma Cuisine*, calls for a chicken to be floured, coated with egg and bread crumbs, and cooked in clarified butter until golden brown. This is put on a serving plate with sweet corn fritters, potato croquettes, bacon and banana, and served with a béchamel sauce to which a little horseradish has been added. M. Escoffier also suggests serving the dish with a tomato sauce!

A more authentic source, a very old Maryland and Virginia cookbook, says the chicken should be dredged with flour and cooked in a skillet in boiling lard about 2½ inches (6 cm) deep and served with a gravy made with drippings from the chicken, flour, milk, and salt and pepper—this to be served with rice. The most delicious dish I have ever eaten under the name of chicken Maryland had a crisp crust on it and was served with a smooth cream gravy and corn fritters. Here is a version that I have found successful.

2 broilers, 2 pounds (900 g) each, split
Lemon juice
2 eggs, beaten
Salt and freshly ground black pepper
1 cup (¼ L) milk

½ pound (225 g) bacon, cut up
1½ to 2 cups (170–225 g) dried bread crumbs
2 tablespoons flour
2 cups (½ L) half-and-half or milk and cream mixed

Rub the chickens well with lemon juice and place in a batter made of the beaten eggs, a little salt and pepper, and the milk. Turn to coat all sides and let stand for 2 hours.

Cook the bacon in a skillet till crisp. Remove the bacon. Dip the soaked chicken pieces in the finely rolled bread crumbs and brown quickly in the hot bacon fat, turning to color evenly. Reduce the heat and cook till tender, about 10 to 12 minutes. Season with salt and pepper to taste.

Remove the chicken from the pan and pour off all the fat except 2 tablespoons. Add the flour, blend with the fat, and cook for 2 or 3 minutes. Add the half-and-half and stir till thickened and smooth. Add salt and pepper to taste.

The traditional way to serve this dish is to arrange the chicken in a bed of the cream sauce and garnish with strips of bacon and corn fritters.

Serves four.

VARIATION
Prepare the chicken as above.

Heat cooking oil or fat in a deep frying kettle to 370°F (185°C). Place the chicken in the frying basket and immerse in the hot fat. Unless you have a huge kettle, it is wise to cook one or two pieces at a time. The entire chicken should cook in 8 to 11 minutes, according to weight and size.

Drain on paper towels and serve with a rich béchamel sauce (see page 179) and corn fritters.

Virginia Fried Chicken with Browned Gravy

This recipe comes from Edna Lewis's book, *A Taste of Country Cooking.*

1 cup (140 g) all-purpose
    unbleached flour
1 cup (140 g) whole-wheat
    flour
1 tablespoon salt
1 teaspoon freshly ground
    black pepper
2 chickens, 2¼ to 2½
    pounds (1015–
    1125 g) each, cut into
    8 pieces each

½ cup (115 g) lard, at
    room temperature
8 tablespoons (115 g)
    butter, at room
    temperature
1 slice smoked ham, cut in
    julienne (optional)

Combine the two flours and add the salt and pepper; mix well. After the chickens have been rinsed and cut into serving pieces, wipe them lightly with a damp cloth. Reserve the backs and wing tips for the stock, which should be started at this point (see below). Roll each piece of chicken in the flour mixture and place the coated pieces on a wide platter or a sheet of waxed paper. Leave the floured pieces to rest for an hour or so to allow time for the flour to adhere to the chicken, avoiding loose flour falling into the frying pan.

To fry the chicken, heat the skillet hot and add the lard. When the lard nearly begins to smoke, add chicken pieces, butter, and ham. Cover and cook on a brisk flame, cooking each side to a good golden color, 10 to 12 minutes on each side. Remove the cooked pieces from the skillet, drain on paper towels, and serve piping hot with gravy.

Serves five to six.

GRAVY

3 chicken backs, plus any
     wing tips and feet
1 stalk celery with leaves
1 thick slice of onion
3 cups (¾ L) cold water

Fat from the skillet
3 rounded tablespoons flour
Salt and freshly ground
     black pepper

Prepare the stock in advance with the chicken backs, celery, onion, and water in a saucepan. Put on a medium burner to cook for 1 hour, gently but continuously. When cooked enough, strain and set aside to cool and skim off the fat. When the chicken is halfway through cooking, spoon out about 4 or 5 tablespoons (55–70 g) of fat from the pan in which it is cooking into a 9-inch (23 cm) skillet, add the flour, and set over a medium flame. Stir until the pan heats up and the flour turns a dark chestnut brown. Remove the skillet from the burner and add 2½ cups (6 dL) chicken stock. Stir well and return the skillet to the burner. Bring to a simmer and cook gently for 15 minutes. Season to taste with salt and pepper. If the gravy is too thick, add more stock or plain water. Remove any excess fat that rises to the top of the gravy.

Pan-Fried Chicken

1 fryer, 2½ to 3 pounds,
     (1125–1350 g), cut
     into 8 pieces
Flour for dredging
Salt and freshly ground
     black pepper

Lard for frying
1 cup (¼ L) heavy cream,
     blended with 2 egg
     yolks

Dredge the chicken pieces heavily with flour, salt, and pepper. Let stand on a rack for 30 minutes or longer. Melt ½ to ¾ inch (1¼–2 cm) of lard in a skillet, and when it is very hot, brown the chicken pieces quickly on all sides. Do not crowd the pan. If necessary, brown a few pieces at a time and transfer to a platter lined with paper towels in a 300°F (150°C) oven while you continue cooking. When all the chicken is browned, arrange in the skillet, reduce the heat, and cover. Allow to cook for 20 to 25 minutes. After 10 minutes, rearrange the pieces to bring the white meat to the top; and after 15 to 20 minutes, remove the white meat to a hot platter and keep warm.

When all the chicken is done, remove from the pan and pour off all but 1 tablespoon fat. Add the cream mixed with the egg yolks and stir over low heat till thickened; do not allow to boil. Season to taste. Pour over the chicken and serve at once.

Serves four.

VARIATION

Clay Triplette's Pan-Fried Chicken: Dredge the chicken with flour, 1 teaspoon salt, 1 teaspoon freshly ground black pepper, and ¼ teaspoon cinnamon. Brown on all sides in 1 cup shortening, reduce the heat, and cook for 10 minutes. Cover, and cook the white meat for 5 minutes more, the dark meat for 10 minutes.

Chicken Kiev

12 tablespoons (170 g) butter
2 tablespoons chopped parsley
1½ teaspoons dried tarragon
1 clove garlic, crushed
Salt and freshly ground black pepper to taste

6 whole chicken breasts, cut in half, boned, and skinned
Seasoned flour for dredging
3 or 4 eggs, beaten
Fresh bread crumbs
Cooking oil or clarified butter for deep frying

Soften the butter in a bowl and mix with the herbs, garlic, and seasonings. Form into 12 fingers and freeze until firm, about 45 minutes.

Wash the chicken breasts and pat dry. With a mallet or meat pounder, flatten the breasts between two sheets of waxed paper. Place a finger of butter in the center of each chicken piece. Roll the chicken around the butter, tucking in the ends to seal well. Roll each breast in seasoned flour. Dip into beaten egg, and then into bread crumbs to coat. Place on a piece of foil and freeze or chill for 1 hour. To cook, fry the breasts in deep oil or clarified butter for about 5 to 6 minutes, or until crisp and brown. Drain and serve immediately.

Serves twelve.

Stuffed Breast of Chicken with Mushroom Sauce

This is a recipe from the files of one of America's famous restaurant chains, Schrafft's. It makes a good dish for a dinner party or buffet.

4 whole chicken breasts, cut in half, boned, and poached in butter
3 cups (170 g) sliced mushroom caps, sautéed (reserve the stems)
1 1/2 tablespoons finely chopped onion
2 tablespoons chopped parsley
1/4 cup (30 g) dried bread crumbs

FOR THE SAUCE
8 tablespoons (115 g) butter
1/2 cup (70 g) flour
1/2 cup (1 dL) milk, scalded
1/4 cup (1/2 dL) heavy cream

1/4 cup (1/2 dL) heavy cream
Salt and freshly ground black pepper
Flour for dredging
Finely rolled cracker crumbs
2 eggs, beaten
Fresh bread crumbs
10 tablespoons (145 g) clarified butter for frying

2 cups (1/2 L) rich chicken stock
1/2 cup (1 dL) mushroom liquor (see below)
1/4 cup (1/2 dL) or more Madeira

Cut a pocket in each of the cooked chicken breasts. Prepare a filling with two-thirds of the sautéed mushrooms, the onion, parsley, dried bread crumbs, heavy cream, and salt and pepper to taste. Stuff the breasts with this mixture.

Flour the stuffed breasts, roll in fine cracker crumbs, dip in beaten egg seasoned with salt and pepper, and finally roll in fresh bread crumbs. Quickly brown in clarified butter and serve with the following sauce:

Prepare a mushroom liquor by cooking the reserved mushroom stems in water to cover for 10 minutes. Strain and set aside. Melt the butter in a saucepan, and blend in the flour. Cook for a minute or 2, then add the scalded milk, heavy cream, and chicken stock. Cook, stirring constantly, till well thickened. Add the mushroom liquor, the remaining sautéed mushrooms, and the Madeira. Correct the seasoning. Stir until blended and heated through.

Serves eight.

Chicken Panné

4 whole chicken breasts, cut in half and boned
Flour
2 eggs, beaten
Fresh bread crumbs
6 tablespoons (85 g) butter

Salt and freshly ground black pepper
3 tablespoons Cognac, warmed
1 cup (¼ L) cream, blended with 2 egg yolks

Put the boned breasts between two sheets of waxed paper and pound quite flat with a heavy cleaver or meat pounder. Dip in the flour, beaten egg, and bread crumbs, in that order. Refrigerate until ready to use.

To cook, heat the butter in a skillet over a high flame until bubbling, but not smoking. Add the chicken breasts, two at a time, and brown quickly for a couple of minutes on both sides, sprinkling with salt and pepper, and transferring to a hot platter as they are done. Return to the pan and, off-heat, flame with the Cognac. Remove to the hot platter and keep warm. To the skillet, add the cream-egg mixture and stir over medium heat until just thickened, making sure it does not come to a boil. Correct the seasoning and serve with chicken.

Serves eight.

POACHED CHICKEN

Poached chicken can be a delicious dish, especially when it is treated like the *poule au pot* of France or the *pollo bollito* of Italy. But it requires careful simmering—the merest bubbling. If you allow it to boil away, you will have overcooked meat and all the flavor will have drained into the broth. Remove the chicken when it is just tender and cook the broth down for a richer flavor. If you stuff the bird, be sure the vent is well sewn up and covered or the broth will seep in and make the stuffing soggy.

Poached chicken can be served either hot or cold. If serving cold, allow it to cool to room temperature. It will taste far better than if it has been touched by the rigor mortis of refrigeration.

Poached Chicken with Dumplings

1 roasting chicken, 5 to 6
    pounds (2¼–2¾ kg)
½ lemon
Several sprigs of parsley
1 bay leaf
1 medium onion, stuck with
    2 or 3 cloves
8 peppercorns

Dash of freshly grated
    nutmeg
Salt to taste
Cold water to cover
Either of the two dumpling
    recipes below
Chopped parsley

Rub the chicken, inside and out, with the half lemon. Put the parsley sprigs in the cavity of the chicken and truss (see page 38). Place in a deep kettle with the bay leaf, onion, peppercorns, nutmeg, and salt to taste. Cover with cold water, place over medium-high heat, and bring to a boil. Remove the scum, reduce the heat, and cover tightly. Simmer until tender, about 45 to 60 minutes. Do not overcook or you will have a stringy mess. Remove the chicken to a hot platter and keep warm. Strain the broth, return to the pot, and let it cook down over high heat. Then cook the dumplings in the broth. You may serve the broth first, followed by the chicken and dumplings, both sprinkled with chopped parsley.

Serves four to six.

Light Dumplings

2 cups (285 g) flour
4½ teaspoons baking
    powder

¼ teaspoon salt
1 cup (¼ L) milk

Sift together the flour and baking powder. Combine all the ingredients and toss together lightly with a fork. Drop by spoonfuls into boiling broth. Cover the pan tightly and allow to cook for 13 minutes to the dot.

Nellie Cox's Dumplings

Nellie Cox belonged to the American school of cookery that created hearty, honest food.

2 cups (285 g) flour
2 tablespoons (30 g) butter

Salt to taste
Water as needed

Mix the flour, butter and salt, adding enough water to make a stiff dough. Roll out to the thickness of ⅛ inch (⅓ cm). Cut in pieces 1 x 3 inches (2½ x 7½ cm). Drop into boiling broth and cook for 20 minutes, uncovered, stirring frequently to keep them from sticking.

Poached Chicken with Rice

1 large roasting chicken,
    4 to 5 pounds (1¾–
    2¼ kg)
½ lemon
1 onion, stuck with 3 cloves
Few sprigs of parsley

1 carrot
Pinch of dried thyme
Cold water to cover
Salt to taste
1 cup (170 g) raw rice

Rub the chicken, inside and out, with the half lemon. Put the onion, parsley, carrot, and thyme in the cavity of the chicken and truss (see page 38). Place in a deep kettle, cover with cold water, and bring to a boil. Remove the scum, then reduce the heat, add salt to taste, and cover tightly. Simmer until just tender, about 50 to 60 minutes. Remove the chicken and cook down the broth. Before doing so, draw off 2 cups (½ L) of the broth.

Combine with the rice in a small, heavy pot, cover, and simmer for 15 minutes, or until tender. (The rice can also be cooked in the pot while the broth reduces.) Return the chicken to the kettle and correct the seasoning. Serve with the rice and broth. Serves four.

Chicken in the Pot

This is a version of the French dish known to the world as *poule au pot*. It is the custom in France to eat bowls of the broth followed by the chicken.

1 large roasting chicken, 4
 to 5 pounds (1¾–
 2¼ kg), liver and
 gizzard reserved
½ lemon
½ pound (225 g) sausage
 meat
2 medium onions, finely
 chopped
1 medium clove garlic,
 chopped
1½ cups (170 g) dry bread
 crumbs

1 tablespoon chopped
 parsley
Pinch of dried thyme
Salt and freshly ground
 black pepper to taste
6 egg yolks, beaten
Crust of old bread
1 pound (450 g) beef shin
1 pound (450 g) veal neck
Salt pork or bacon
Cold water to cover

Rub the interior of the chicken with half a lemon. Stuff it with the following mixture:

Fry the sausage meat in a skillet till it is rendered of its fat. Pour off most of the fat and add the onions and garlic. Let this cook a few minutes before adding the bread crumbs. Mix well and add the reserved liver and gizzard chopped, and the parsley, thyme, and salt and pepper. Remove from the heat and let cool. Add the beaten egg yolks. Mix thoroughly with the hands and stuff the bird, but not too tightly. Place a crust of old bread over the vent and sew it up securely. Tie the neck skin and truss the bird (see page 38). Place in a large pot with beef shin, veal neck, and a small piece of salt pork or bacon (see variation). Cover with cold water, bring to a boil, and skim. Reduce the heat, cover, and simmer till the chicken is tender, about 50 to

60 minutes. Remove the chicken to cool. Reduce the broth by one-third until you have one that is rich and strong. Skim off the fat. Serve the hot broth in bowls, and follow with the cooled chicken and the stuffing, which may be removed and sliced. Serve with a good mustard mayonnaise and salad.

Serves four.

VARIATION

Carrots and onions may be added to the broth while it is cooking, and then may be served with the soup. You may also flavor the broth with parsley, thyme, and rosemary.

Poached Chicken Farm Style

1 large boiling fowl, 4 to 5
  pounds (1¾–2¼ kg)
½ lemon
Stuffing of your choice (see
  pages 169–175)
Crust of old bread
Cold water to cover
6 medium onions, peeled
6 to 8 carrots

A sprig or two of parsley
Salt to taste
6 to 8 small turnips, peeled
Potatoes, peeled
1 cup (¼ L) heavy cream,
  blended with 2 egg
  yolks
Freshly ground black pepper

Rub the fowl, inside and out, with the half lemon. Remove the fowl's wing ends, but add to the pot. Fill the chicken with the stuffing of your choice and sew up the vent securely, having covered the stuffing with an old crust of bread before closing the vent. Sew up the skin at the neck end of the bird and fasten securely with a skewer. Truss. Place in a kettle with cold water to cover. Bring to a boil, skim, and reduce the heat. Cover tightly and simmer 1 hour. Add the onions, carrots, a sprig or two of parsley, and salt to taste and continue simmering for another 1 to 1½ hours. Then add the turnips and 1 or 2 potatoes per person. When tender, remove chicken and continue cooking the vegetables till they are done.

Remove 2 cups (½ L) of the broth, strain and degrease and combine with the cream and egg yolks. Stir over low heat till well thickened, but do not allow to boil. Add salt and pepper to taste. Place chicken on a hot platter and remove all strings and skewers. Arrange the vegetables around it and serve with the sauce.

Serves four.

Poached Chicken with Spaghetti

1 large roasting chicken,
    about 5 or 6 pounds
    (2¼ to 2¾ kg)
½ lemon
1 onion, stuck with 3 cloves
3 sprigs parsley
1 sprig fresh thyme
3 leaves fresh sweet basil
Cold water to cover
Salt and freshly ground
    black pepper
1 large onion, finely
    chopped

2 cloves garlic, chopped
2 tablespoons (30 g) butter
2 cans (each 1 pound; or
    450 g) Italian
    tomatoes
2 tablespoons chopped
    parsley
1½ pounds (675 g)
    spaghetti
Freshly grated Parmesan
    cheese

Rub the interior of the chicken with half a lemon. Fill the cavity with the onion stuck with the cloves, 3 parsley sprigs, thyme sprig, and 2 leaves of sweet basil. Cover with cold water; bring to a boil and skim. Salt and pepper to taste, reduce heat, cover, and simmer until tender, about 50 to 60 minutes. Remove the meat from the bones and reserve; return the carcass to the pot and simmer till the broth is reduced by half.

Sauté the chopped onion and garlic in the butter. Add the Italian tomatoes and cook down until thickened. Add the remaining basil and 2 tablespoons chopped parsley. Season with salt and pepper to taste. Mix this with the chicken meat, and add the chicken broth after removing the carcass. Simmer over a very low flame for 30 minutes.

Cook the spaghetti in boiling, salted water till *al dente*. Drain and remove to a large bowl. Ladle the sauce and chicken over the pasta and sprinkle liberally with Parmesan cheese. Serve with plenty of French or Italian bread and red wine.

Serves eight.

Djaj M'Kalli

This is an interesting poached chicken dish from North Africa.

3 chickens, 3 pounds
   (1350 g) each
2 tablespoons coarse salt
6 cloves garlic
1 cup (¼ L) vegetable oil
2 teaspoons ground ginger
1 teaspoon turmeric
1 teaspoon black pepper
Good pinch of saffron

3 large onions, grated
8 tablespoons (115 g)
   butter
2 cups (½ L) water
2 cups (½ L) chicken stock
1 pound (450 g) soft ripe
   olives
A few slices of pickled
   lemon (see below)

Start this chicken dish the day before. Wash and drain the chickens and remove all fat from them, then rub them well with a mixture of coarse salt and 3 of the garlic cloves chopped. Let stand 1 hour; wipe off. Rub with a mixture of vegetable oil, ginger, turmeric, black pepper, and saffron. Put in a large bowl with any remaining oil mixture; cover and refrigerate overnight.

Next day, put the chickens in a very large pot with the onions, butter, the 3 remaining cloves of garlic (finely chopped), water, and chicken stock. Bring to a boil, reduce the heat, cover, and simmer until the chickens are tender, 40 to 45 minutes. Remove the chickens and rapidly boil the broth down to a thick, rich sauce, stirring often. Correct seasoning. Add the soft ripe olives and a few slices of pickled lemon. Carve the chickens and return to the simmering sauce to reheat. Serve with saffron rice.

Serves ten to twelve.

Pickled Lemons

8 large lemons
½ cup (100 g) coarse salt

Olive oil or half olive oil
   and half peanut oil

Slice the lemons ½ inch (1½ cm) thick, and place in a colander. Cover with salt, and wrap the colander with plastic wrap. Let stand for 24 hours. Remove the wrap, rinse the lemon well, and arrange in fruit jars or other jars with covers. Add enough oil to completely cover the slices. Cover and let stand for 1 to 2 weeks before using.

Pickled lemons will keep indefinitely if kept covered with oil. If additional salt is needed after the slices have ripened, add 1 tablespoon of salt to each jar.

Creole Chicken

This recipe, while not strictly a poached chicken, seems to belong here rather than with the casserole dishes. It is a hearty, flavorful dish, suitable for a large family or for a buffet. Choose a bird that can take long, slow cooking.

1 large poaching fowl, 5 to 6 pounds (2¼ to 2¾ kg), cut up
Flour for dredging
6 tablespoons (85 g) clarified butter
4 large onions, finely chopped
1 stalk celery, finely chopped
2/3 cup (40 g) chopped parsley
3 green peppers, seeded and finely chopped
5 cloves garlic, chopped
1½ cups (3½ dL) tomato purée
½ teaspoon crushed rosemary leaves
1 tablespoon paprika
¼ teaspoon cayenne
2 teaspoons salt
1 teaspoon freshly ground black pepper
1 tablespoon sweet chili powder
1 bay leaf, crushed
Boiling water or stock to cover

Dredge the chicken pieces in flour and brown quickly in the butter in a large skillet. Transfer the chicken to a deep kettle, leaving the butter in the skillet. Add the chopped onion, celery, parsley, green pepper, and garlic and sauté until the onion softens. Beforehand, these vegetables may be put through a coarse chopper or food processor if you wish. Scoop out in spoonfuls and place on the chicken in the kettle. Add a little hot water to the skillet, rinse well and add to the kettle. Add the tomato purée seasoned with the rosemary, paprika, cayenne, salt, black pepper, sweet chili powder, and crushed bay leaf.

Add enough boiling water or stock to cover the chicken and stir briskly over a hot fire till the liquid boils. Reduce the heat and simmer slowly until the chicken is very tender, and the sauce reaches a velvety smoothness (see note below). Cooking time varies from 3 to 4 hours. Serve with boiled rice or spoon-bread.

Serves eight for a buffet supper dish or six for a dinner.

VARIATION

If you wish, remove the chicken and thicken the sauce with a roux made with ¾ cup (110 g) flour and 8 tablespoons (115 g) butter.

BROILED CHICKEN

Broiling chickens weigh from 1½ to 3 pounds (675–1350 g) and are usually served split in half or quartered, depending on size. It is best to remove the necks and backbones and flatten slightly before broiling. Be sure to preheat the broiler and rub the broiler pan rack with butter or oil.

Basic Broiled Chicken

Brush the chicken halves or quarters well with butter or oil. Place on a greased rack, skin side down, and broil about 4 inches from moderate heat for 12 to 14 minutes, depending on the size of the chicken. Brush with butter if it seems too dry. Season with salt and pepper, turn skin side up, and brush again with butter. Continue to broil gently, basting once or twice, for another 12 to 14 minutes. Test for tenderness with a fork; or pierce the thigh joint with a thin, sharp knife. If the juices run slightly pink (my preference) or clear, the chicken is done.

Broiled Chicken with Rosemary Butter

2 teaspoons chopped fresh
    rosemary or 1 teaspoon
    dried, crushed
1 tablespoon finely chopped
    parsley
1 tablespoon finely minced
    chives
Salt and freshly ground
    black pepper

8 tablespoons (115 g)
    softened butter
1½ teaspoons lemon juice
¼ cup (15 g) bread
    crumbs, toasted
1 broiler, split

Preheat the broiler. Blend the herbs, seasonings, and butter. Rub the chicken well with one-half the blended butter. Place skin side down on a greased broiler rack and broil, 4 inches from moderate heat, for 12 to 14 minutes. Turn, brush with more butter, and broil, skin side up, for another 12 to 14 minutes. Sprinkle with the bread crumbs a minute or 2 before it is done. Serve with the remaining butter.

Serves two.

Leonie de Sounin's Herbed Broilers

This recipe is from Leonie de Sounin's book *Magic with Herbs*.

2 small broilers or fryers, about 1½ pounds (675 g) each, left whole
½ lemon
2 tablespoons chopped parsley
1 teaspoon chopped, fresh rosemary or ½ teaspoon dried, crushed

1 tablespoon chopped chives
Pinch of ground ginger
6 tablespoons (85 g) softened butter
Salt to taste
4 strips bacon

Preheat the broiler.

Rub the chickens inside and out with half a lemon. Thoroughly blend the herbs and ginger with the butter and a bit of salt. Spread the herbed butter under the breast and thigh skin of the chickens. This will keep the meat juicy and impart an unbelievably good flavor to the bird as it cooks. Arrange the birds on their sides on a greased rack in a broiling pan and cover each with 2 strips of bacon. Broil under moderate heat for 5 minutes 4 inches from the heating unit. Turn, rearrange the bacon strips, and broil for another five minutes. Then place in the oven and roast at 400°F (205°C) until brown and tender, about 15 to 20 minutes. Split in half and serve.

Serves four.

VARIATION

Combine 1 cup (¼ L) olive oil or vegetable oil, the juice of a lemon, 1 tablespoon chopped fresh tarragon or 1½ teaspoons dried, 2 tablespoons chopped parsley, 1 tablespoon chopped chives, a pinch of dried thyme, salt and freshly ground black pepper. Pour over the chicken in a bowl, and let marinate for at least 12 hours, turning several times. Remove the chickens from the marinade, dry with paper towels, and arrange on their sides on a rack in a broiling pan. Broil as directed above.

Chicken Teriyaki

2 broilers split
½ cup (1 dL) olive or
    peanut oil
2/3 cup (1½ dL) Japanese
    soy sauce
2 tablespoons grated fresh
    ginger or 1 tablespoon
    chopped candied gin-
    ger, washed free of all
    sugar

2 cloves garlic, finely
    chopped
1 tablespoon grated tan-
    gerine or orange rind
¼ cup (½ dL) sherry

Place the chicken in a shallow pan. Blend all the remaining ingredients well and pour over the chicken. Turn the halves several times while they marinate, anywhere from an hour to 24 hours.

Preheat the broiler. Place the chicken a little further from the heating unit than usual—at least 6 to 9 inches (15–23 cm)—to prevent the soy sauce from caramelizing. Broil bone side up, for 12 to 14 minutes, brushing once or twice with the marinade. Then turn carefully, brush again with marinade, and broil for another 12 to 14 minutes while continuing to baste.

Serves four.

Deviled Broilers

Broil chickens as directed in basic recipe, page 32. Just before they are ready to be served, remove from the broiler and sprinkle the skin side with hot buttered bread crumbs. Place in a hot oven for a few minutes to crisp the crumbs. Serve with the following sauce (enough for 4 to 6 servings):

1 onion, finely chopped
2 cloves garlic, finely
   chopped
6 tablespoons (85 g) butter
   or bacon fat
1 cup (¼ L) tomato sauce
2 tablespoons Worcester-
   shire sauce

½ teaspoon dry mustard
Giblets from the chickens,
   chopped and poached
   until tender
Salt and freshly ground
   black pepper to taste
Chopped parsley

In a skillet, sauté the onion and garlic in the butter or bacon fat.
When transparent, add the tomato sauce, Worcestershire sauce,
dry mustard, chopped giblets, and salt and pepper. Blend thoroughly and allow to simmer for 5 minutes. At the last minute
stir in the degreased juices from the broiling pan. Add chopped
parsley and serve with the crusty broilers.

Deviled Squab Chicken with Sauce Béarnaise

6 squab chickens, about 1
   to 1½ pounds (450–
   675 g) each, split
½ cup (1 dL) soy sauce
½ cup (1 dL) sherry
2 tablespoons Dijon
   mustard
1 tablespoon Tabasco
½ cup (1 dL) olive oil
1 cup (¼ L) melted butter,
   or as needed

3 cups (170 g) bread
   crumbs, toasted, or as
   needed
1½ teaspoons freshly
   ground black pepper
Fresh watercress for garnish
Sauce béarnaise (see page
   181)

Marinate the chickens for 2 hours, turning often, in a mixture of
the soy sauce, sherry, mustard, Tabasco, and oil. Preheat the
broiler. Broil, skin side down for 6 to 8 minutes, then turn and
broil another 6 minutes. Remove from the broiler, dip in melted
butter, and roll in the bread crumbs mixed with the pepper. Return to the broiler for 2 minutes; watch carefully. Turn, brush
with butter, and broil another 2 minutes. Garnish with fresh
watercress and serve with the sauce béarnaise.
   Serves six.

Stuffed Broiled Chicken Breasts

2 whole chicken breasts, split	¼ cup (30 g) chopped chives or green onions
6 tablespoons (85 g) butter	1 teaspoon dried basil
¼ cup (15 g) chopped parsley	Heavy cream
	Salt and freshly ground black pepper

Preheat the broiler.

Using a thin-bladed sharp knife, make a small pocket in each of the breasts. Cream the butter with the parsley, chives or green onions, and basil. Stuff the chicken breasts with this mixture and secure the opening with a toothpick. Brush the breasts with additional butter and broil under moderate heat for 10 to 12 minutes, turning once, starting bone side up. Just before they are finished, brush them with heavy cream and sprinkle with salt and pepper.

Serve with tiny new potatoes dressed with crumbled bacon. Serves four.

Barbecue Chicken

3 to 4 broilers, split	½ cup (1 dL) honey
2 medium onions, chopped	½ cup (1 dL) rich broth or stock
¼ cup (½ dL) olive oil	¼ cup (½ dL) Worcestershire sauce
1 cup (¼ L) Italian tomato purée	1 teaspoon dry mustard
1 teaspoon salt	½ cup (1 dL) dry red wine
1 teaspoon dried basil	

Sauté the onion in the olive oil until soft. Add all the rest of the ingredients except the chicken and wine and simmer gently for 10 to 15 minutes. Add the wine and heat through. Cool. Marinate the chicken halves in this mixture for 2 to 3 hours, turning them frequently to be sure they are well bathed.

Meanwhile prepare a charcoal fire. Place the chicken halves on a rack 3 to 4 inches (8–10 cm) from the coals and charcoal broil. Arrange bone side down and broil for 12 to 15 minutes. Brush with sauce, turn, and broil for another 12 to 15 minutes.

Test for doneness by puncturing the thigh joint with a fork. When the juice runs clear or slightly pink, not red, the chicken is cooked. Do not overcook, or it will be dry and tasteless.

Serves six to eight.

ROAST CHICKEN

Many of us remember the days when stuffed roasted chicken was the piece de résistance of every Sunday's midday dinner, and we spent uncomfortable afternoons after eating too much of it. Nowadays it is everyday fare, but a roasted chicken still makes a elegant dish if it is perfectly cooked. I like to turn mine as it roasts to help keep the juices circulated and the skin evenly browned. It can be roasted either with or without stuffing. In either case it should be trussed.

Roasting chickens weigh anywhere fom 4 to 6 pounds (1¾–2¾ kg), although the larger ones are hard to find. A bird of 4 to 5 pounds (1¾–2¼ kg) will be ample for four people. It should take 1 to 1¼ hours to cook. Wipe the chicken with a damp cloth and rub the cavity with half a lemon. If not stuffing, place a chunk—3 to 4 tablespoons (45–60 g) of butter—inside and sprinkle with salt. Truss, as directed below. (If stuffing, fill the chicken lightly and close the vent with a skewer or seal with a piece of folded foil; proceed to truss.) Rub the skin generously with softened butter. Place on its side on a rack in a roasting pan. Roast for 20 minutes at 425°F (220°C). Turn on its other side, brush with melted butter, and roast for another 20 minutes. Then turn breast side up, brush with the pan juices, and salt and pepper well. Roast for a final 20 minutes. Prick the thigh joint to see if the juices run clear—don't be afraid of a little pinkness. Return to the oven, if necessary. If done, transfer to a hot platter or a carving board, and allow to settle for about 10 minutes before carving or cutting into quarters.

VARIATIONS

With bacon: Instead of buttering the chicken, drape it with rashers of bacon, moving them to the top each time you turn the bird. Baste the skin with a combination of butter and bacon drippings.

With herbed butter: To 8 tablespoons (115 g) of softened butter add the herb of your choice—2 tablespoons parsley, 2 tablespoons chives, 1 tablespoon fresh tarragon (or 1 teaspoon dried), or a combination of herbs. Blend well and spread under the loosened skin of the breast and thighs. Also put a tablespoon or so in the cavity if it is not stuffed.

STUFFING I

6 tablespoons (85 g) butter,
    more if needed
1 onion, chopped
½ cup (60 g) chopped
    celery
¼ cup (15 g) chopped
    parsley

1 teaspoon dried thyme
Salt and freshly ground
    black pepper
2½ cups (140 g) fine fresh
    bread crumbs

Melt the butter in a skillet, add the onion, and sauté until just soft. Add the rest of the ingredients and toss. If too dry, add more melted butter.

STUFFING II

Use a tarragon-flavored bread stuffing in the body cavity (see page 170). Reduce the quantity according to the size of your bird. Use well-flavored sausage meat to stuff the neck cavity. This two-stuffing arrangement would work best with an especially large roasting chicken.

TRUSSING

Trussing the chicken or game bird is the process of tying it and skewering it before placing it in the oven. It tends to keep the bird in a compact shape during the process of cooking. Fold the wings back so the tips are under the back. Press the legs and thighs close to the body and secure with a skewer or two run into the body of the bird. Tie string around the ends of the legs and around the tail and leave two equally long pieces of string. Carry the string around the wings, cross it in the middle of the back, and tie it securely over the breast. Always remove all string and skewers before carving and serving.

Giblet Sauce for Roast Chicken

3 tablespoons fat from the
   roasting pan
3 tablespoons flour
1½ cups (3½ dL) hot
   chicken broth (made
   from the giblets and
   neck) or milk, or as
   needed

Giblets, cooked and
   chopped
Salt and freshly ground
   black pepper to taste

Pour off all but 3 tablespoons fat from the roasting pan. Place
the pan over low heat, add the flour, and blend. Cook for 2 or 3
minutes. Add the heated broth or milk, scrape in all the brown
residue in the pan, and stir until thickened. If too thick add a
little more broth or milk. Add the chopped giblets, season to
taste, and let cook for a few minutes more.

VARIATION
Tarragon Sauce: Make the sauce with fat, flour, and 1 cup of
chicken or veal broth, as directed above. Add 1 tablespoon
chopped fresh tarragon or 1 teaspoon dried tarragon. Then stir
in ¾ cup (1¾ dL) heavy cream over low heat until smooth.
Season to taste, and stir in 1 tablespoon chopped parsley.

Roast Chicken Sesame

3 pounds (1350 g) chicken
   parts
Flour for dredging
1 egg, beaten with a little
   water
1 cup (115 g) sesame seeds
16 tablespoons (225 grams)
   butter

¼ cup (½ dL) Cognac,
   warmed
¾ cup (1¾ dL) dry white
   wine
¾ cup (1¾ dL) heavy
   cream

Dredge the chicken pieces well in flour, dip in beaten egg, and
roll in sesame seeds till completely covered. Brown quickly in
8 tablespoons (115 g) butter. Transfer the pieces to a large
flame-proof casserole, pour the Cognac over and flambé.
   Roast, uncovered, in a 325°F (165°C) oven for 45 minutes

to 1 hour, basting occasionally with a mixture of wine and the remaining butter, melted. Remove from the oven. Add the cream
to the pan, blend with the pan juices, and baste the chicken well.
Return to the oven and cook for 20 minutes more.

Serve with crisp fried potatoes and a cucumber, onion, and
tomato salad.

Serves four to six.

Roast Squab Chicken with Curried Rice

This may also be prepared with fresh Cornish game hens.

1 heaping cup (170 g) raw rice, washed	Celery seeds
1 large onion, finely chopped	Chopped parsley
	Salt and freshly ground pepper
6 tablespoons (85 g) butter	1 teaspoon sugar
1 to 3 teaspoons good-quality curry powder, to taste	4 squab chickens, about 1 to 1½ pounds (450–675 g) each
Dash of cayenne	½ cup (1 dL) light cream

Cook the rice in salted water until just tender. Set aside. Sauté
the onion in butter. When soft, stir in curry powder to taste. Add
a dash of cayenne, a few celery seeds, chopped parsley, salt, and
pepper to taste and the sugar. Combine with the rice.

Stuff each chicken with the curried rice; truss securely (see
page 38). Place in a buttered baking dish and brown in a hot
oven (425°F; 220°C). Reduce the heat to 300°F (150°C),
pour cream over the chickens, and bake until quite tender, about
45 minutes.

Serves two to four.

BRAISED CHICKEN, FRICASSEES, CASSEROLES

Braised Stuffed Chicken

8 ounces (225 g) noodles
8 tablespoons (115 g)
    butter, approximately
Salt and freshly ground
    black pepper to taste
¼ pound (115 g) chicken
    livers, chopped
¼ pound (115 g) mush-
    rooms, chopped
½ teaspoon freshly grated
    nutmeg

½ cup (45 g) freshly grated
    Parmesan cheese
½ cup (1 dL) heavy cream
1 tablespoon chopped
    parsley
1 roasting chicken, 4
    pounds (1¾ kg)
1 cup chicken broth

Cook the noodles in boiling salted water just until tender. Drain
and toss with a bit of butter to keep from sticking together.

Sauté the chopped livers and mushrooms in 2 tablespoons (30
g) butter over low heat for 3 minutes. Add to the noodles, along
with the nutmeg, grated cheese, cream, parsley, and salt and
pepper, and blend well. Gently stuff the chicken, sew up the
vent, and truss (see page 38). If there is any extra stuffing, place
it in a small baking dish, dot with butter, and cook with the
chicken for 10 to 15 minutes.

Preheat the oven to 350°F (175°C).

Heat the remaining butter in an ovenproof casserole and
brown the chicken quickly, turning on all sides in the casserole
to achieve an evenness of color. Add the chicken broth and cover
the casserole. Place in the preheated oven and cook for 1½
hours, basting every 20 minutes with a little broth. Serve with
the degreased pan juices; or if you prefer a thickened sauce,
melt 2 tablespoons (30 g) butter in a saucepan and stir in 2
tablespoons flour. Allow to cook for a moment, then add the degreased pan juices and ½ cup (1 dL) milk. Stir over a medium
flame till the sauce thickens, adding more milk if necessary. Season with salt and pepper to taste.

Serves four to six.

Braised Lemon Chicken

1 roasting chicken, 4 pounds
  (1 ¾ kg)
2 ½ lemons
2 tablespoons olive oil
1 large onion, finely
  chopped
2 teaspoons turmeric

2 cups (½ L) chicken broth
  or water
2 cans (1 pound; 450 g)
  chick-peas or gar-
  banzos, drained
4 cloves garlic, crushed
Salt and freshly ground
  black pepper

Rub the chicken inside and out with half a lemon. Heat the oil
in a deep braising pan or Dutch oven. Sauté the onion in the
oil until soft and golden. Sprinkle with half the turmeric and
mix well. Rub the chicken with the remaining turmeric.

Sear the chicken in the oil with the onions, turning it so that
it colors a rather deep yellow on all sides. Add the broth or water,
the drained chick-peas, juice of 2 lemons, garlic, and salt and
pepper to taste. Bring to a boil, then reduce the heat and simmer,
covered, for 1 hour or longer, or until the chicken is just tender.
Remove the chicken from the sauce, cut in serving pieces, and
serve with the chick-peas and the sauce.

Serves four to six.

Hungarian Chicken

6 chicken legs with thighs
1 cup (140 g) flour, or as
  needed
2 tablespoons paprika
2 teaspoons salt
½ teaspoon freshly ground
  black pepper
4 tablespoons (60 g) butter,
  or as needed

¼ cup (½ dL) cooking oil,
  or as needed
1 ½ cups (170 g) chopped
  onion
1 cup (¼ L) broth, or as
  needed
1 cup (¼ L) sour cream
1 tablespoon finely cut
  lemon zest

Put the chicken pieces in a bag with the flour, 1 tablespoon
paprika, and salt and pepper; shake well. Heat the butter and oil
in a heavy skillet till quite hot, and brown the chicken pieces
on both sides. Transfer to a piece of foil or paper towels. Add the

onion to the skillet and brown very well, using additional butter and oil if needed. Return the chicken pieces to the pan with the broth and remaining paprika and simmer, covered, till the chicken is just tender, about 20 minutes. If the broth is absorbed, add more. Transfer the chicken to a hot serving dish. Add the sour cream to the pan off heat and stir into the pan juices; heat for 1 minute but do not boil. Pour over the chicken pieces. Sprinkle the lemon zest on top.

Serve with grilled tomatoes and with noodles tossed with butter and crisp croutons.

Serves four to six.

Country Captain

Based on an East Indian curry, this dish owes its name to the term for a native Indian captain in the pay of his English colonizers. The version given here comes from Cecily Brownstone, the Associated Press food columnist.

1 fryer, about 2¼ pounds
    (1015 g)
¼ cup (35 g) flour
1 teaspoon salt
¼ teaspoon freshly ground
    black pepper
4 tablespoons (60 g) butter
1/3 cup (40 g) finely diced
    onion
1/3 cup (40 g) finely diced
    green pepper

1 clove garlic, crushed
1½ teaspoons curry powder
½ teaspoon dried thyme,
    crushed
1 can (1 pound; 450 g)
    stewed tomatoes
3 tablespoons (20 g) dried
    currants, washed and
    drained
Blanched toasted almonds

The chicken should be cut to yield 2 pieces of breast, 2 wings, 2 legs, and 2 second joints. Save the back, wing tips, neck, and giblets for a broth. Dredge the chicken with a mixture of the flour, salt, and pepper. Heat the butter in a large skillet and brown the chicken. Transfer to a hot platter. Add the onion, green pepper, garlic, curry powder, and thyme to the skillet. Stir over low heat and scrape loose the browned residue in the pan. Add the stewed tomatoes, with their liquid. Arrange the chicken in the skillet, skin side up. Cover and cook slowly until tender, about 20 to 30 minutes. Stir the currants into the sauce. Serve topped with the toasted almonds.

Serves four.

VARIATION

For the final cooking, the dish may be baked, covered, in a 325°F (165°C) oven until tender, about 45 minutes.

Coq au Vin

8 tablespoons (115 g) butter
1 fryer, 3 pounds (1350 g), quartered
1 teaspoon salt
½ teaspoon freshly ground black pepper
¼ cup (½ dL) Cognac
1 bottle dry red wine, as needed
Bouquet garni (1 sprig thyme, 1 bay leaf, 1 sprig parsley, 6 peppercorns, tied in cheesecloth)

12 small white onions
3 slices salt pork, cut in ½-inch (1¼ cm) pieces
12 mushroom caps, quartered
Beurre manié—3 tablespoons flour and 3 tablespoons (45 g) butter

Melt 4 tablespoons (60 g) butter in a large, heavy skillet and brown the chicken over medium-high heat, about 5 minutes on each side. Sprinkle with salt and pepper. Drain off the butter, pour the Cognac over the chicken, and flambé. Add enough wine to just cover the chicken, then add the bouquet garni. Cover the pan and simmer for 30 minutes, or until tender. Test the pieces of white meat first, and if done, transfer to a warm platter while the dark meat continues to cook. Remove the bouquet garni.

Meanwhile, melt the remaining butter in another skillet and brown the onions and salt pork. Then cover and cook very slowly for about 20 minutes, or until the onions are tender. Add the mushrooms and cook for another 4 minutes.

When the chicken has been removed from the pan, degrease the sauce and bring to a boil. Add the beurre manié (the flour and butter kneaded together), a bit at a time, until the sauce has thickened slightly. Correct the seasoning. Add the onions, salt pork, and mushrooms to the chicken, and pour the sauce over all.

Serves four.

Brown Fricassee of Chicken

1 roasting chicken, 4 to 5
    pounds (1¾ to 2¼
    kg), cut up
Flour
Salt and freshly ground
    black pepper
4 tablespoons (60 g) butter
1 medium onion, finely
    chopped

1 garlic clove, finely
    chopped
Pinch each of dried thyme
    and marjoram
Boiling chicken broth or
    water to cover
1 cup (¼ L) heavy cream

Dredge chicken pieces with flour, salt, and pepper. Heat the butter in a heavy kettle and brown the onion and garlic. Add the chicken pieces and brown them nicely on all sides. Add the thyme and marjoram. Cover with boiling broth or water and simmer, covered, until tender, about 45 minutes. Add the cream and let it cook down for a few minutes. Correct the seasoning and serve with boiled rice. If you wish a thicker sauce, you may thicken it with beurre manié—small balls of flour and butter blended well.

Serves four to six.

American Fricassee of Chicken

1 roasting chicken, 4 pounds
    (1¾ kg), cut up, neck
    and giblets reserved
6 cups (1½ L) water
1 small veal knuckle
Salt to taste
1 onion
1 sprig parsley
1 sprig fresh thyme
1 bay leaf

2 cloves
3 tablespoons (45 g) butter
3 tablespoons flour
1 cup (¼ L) heavy cream
Freshly ground black pepper
    to taste
Pinch of freshly grated
    nutmeg
Chopped parsley

Combine the neck, wing tips, giblets, veal knuckle, salt, onion, and parsley and thyme sprigs with the water. Simmer for 1 hour. Strain the broth.

Pour the boiling broth over the pieces of chicken in a large kettle. Add the bay leaf and cloves and simmer with the cover on the kettle till the chicken is tender. This should take about 45 minutes.

In a heavy skillet, melt the butter and add the flour. Blend well, then add 2 cups (½ L) of the chicken broth and stir until it begins to thicken. Gradually add the cream, stirring constantly till the mixture is thoroughly blended. Season with salt, pepper, and a pinch of nutmeg. Arrange the pieces of chicken on a hot platter, surround with boiled rice or buttered noodles, and pour the sauce over all. Sprinkle with a little chopped parsley.

Serves four to six.

Blanquette of Chicken

1 roasting chicken, 4 to 5 pounds (1¾ to 2¼ kg), cut up
Boiling chicken broth or water to cover
1 onion, peeled
1 carrot
1 stalk celery
Bouquet garni (parsley, chervil, and marjoram tied in cheesecloth)
Salt and freshly ground black pepper
2 tablespoons (30 g) butter
2 tablespoons flour
1 cup (¼ L) cream, mixed with 2 egg yolks
Lemon juice to taste

Place chicken pieces in a kettle and cover with boiling broth or water. Add the onion, carrot, celery, and bouquet garni. Let simmer until tender, about 1 hour. Add salt and pepper to taste.

When the chicken is tender, remove it to a hot platter or casserole. Make a roux by blending the butter with the flour in a skillet; cook gently, taking care not to brown it. Strain the broth, add to it the roux, and stir till it has thickened. Add the cream blended with the egg yolks and stir constantly till well combined with the sauce. Add a few drops of lemon juice, correct the seasoning, and pour over the chicken. Serve with sautéed mushrooms and boiled rice.

Serves four to six.

Fricassee of Chicken with White Wine

1 roasting chicken, 4 pounds (1¾ kg), cut up
½ lemon
5 tablespoons (70 g) butter
1 pound (450 g) tiny white onions, peeled
½ pound (225 g) sliced mushrooms
Dry white wine to cover
3 or 4 leaves fresh tarragon
Salt and freshly ground black pepper
1 cup (¼ L) cream

Rub each chicken piece with the lemon half and allow to sit for 15 minutes. Gently sauté the chicken pieces in the butter in a deep skillet or casserole till they are a pale golden shade. Add the onions and sliced mushrooms. Pour in enough wine to cover and add the fresh tarragon. Cover and simmer very gently for 45 minutes, or until the chicken is tender. Season with salt and pepper to taste, and just before serving blend the cream well into the sauce. Serve with boiled rice.

Serves four to six.

Paella

For a variation of the Spanish paella, try making it with chicken wings rather than the cut-up whole chicken.

12 chicken wings
Flour
6 tablespoons peanut oil
Salt and freshly ground black pepper to taste
1 onion, finely chopped
2 garlic cloves, chopped
1½ cups (255 g) raw rice
Boiling chicken broth or water to cover
Pinch of saffron
1 or 2 Italian or Spanish sausages, sliced
½ cup (1 dL) chopped canned tomatoes
24 clams, in their shells
12 shrimp, in their shells
3 pimientos, cut in thin strips
½ package (10 ounce size; 285 g) frozen green peas, thawed

Flour the chicken wings, and brown in oil in a large skillet or paella pan. Season with salt and pepper, remove to a platter, and keep warm.

Sauté the onion and garlic in the oil until soft. Add the rice and stir until well coated with oil and translucent. Pour over it enough boiling chicken broth or water to cover, then season with salt, pepper, and saffron and let the liquid cook down. Add the chicken wings, sliced sausages, tomatoes, and additional liquid, if necessary. Simmer over low heat until the rice is just beginning to get tender; add the clams and shrimp. Cook until the shrimp are pink and cooked through and the clam shells open. Nearly all the liquid should have cooked away at this point; if it has not, raise the heat until it evaporates, leaving the rice firm and the grains separate. Garnish with pimiento strips and peas (the heat from the paella will warm them through).

Serves six.

Chicken Calandria

This buffet dish comes from an old Mexican cook, Calandria, who made many pilgrimages to California to prepare and teach her national dishes. She would arrive complete with aprons, *metate*, and all the mysterious ingredients that go into Mexican foods.

1 roasting chicken, 5 pounds (2¼ kg), cut up, or an equivalent amount of chicken breasts and legs
½ cup (60 g) white water-ground cornmeal
½ cup (1 dL) olive oil
3 medium white onions, finely chopped
3 cloves garlic, finely chopped
¾ cup (1¾ dL) dry red wine, heated

Pinch each of mace and dried marjoram
1 teaspoon sesame seeds
½ teaspoon caraway seeds
3 cups boiling water
Salt to taste
1 cup (115 g) whole blanched almonds
1 cup (225 g) pitted green olives
¼ cup (30 g) sweet chili powder

Dredge the pieces of chicken in the cornmeal. Save any cornmeal left behind. Heat the olive oil in a large casserole. When hot but not smoking, sear the chicken slightly on all sides. Lower the heat, add the onion and garlic, and mix well with the chicken. Add the wine, mace, marjoram, sesame seeds, caraway seeds, boiling water, and salt. Cover and allow to simmer gently for 1 hour.

Add the almonds, olives, and chili powder and simmer for another hour, stirring occasionally.

Mix a little of the reserved cornmeal with water and add to thicken the sauce to the desired consistency, stirring continuously to keep the cornmeal from forming lumps or sticking to the bottom of the pot.

Put aside until ready to serve, for this dish is much better reheated.

Serves five to six.

Chicken Casserole with Rice

1 roasting chicken, 3 pounds (1350 g), cut up
½ lemon
Flour for dredging
Salt and freshly ground black pepper
¼ pound (115 g) bacon, cut in slivers

6 carrots, scraped and quartered
3 medium onions, sliced
1 large clove garlic, peeled
1 teaspoon dried tarragon
½ cup (30 g) chopped parsley
1½ cups (255 g) raw rice
Chicken broth as needed

Preheat the oven to 375°F (190°C).

Rub chicken pieces with half a lemon, then dredge with flour, salt, and pepper. Fry the bacon slivers in a skillet till crisp. Remove the bacon and place in an ovenproof casserole. Brown the chicken in the bacon fat left in the skillet, a few pieces at a time so it achieves an even color. Place in the casserole, along with the carrots, sliced onion, garlic, tarragon, and parsley.

Brown the rice in the skillet, adding more fat if necessary. Add this to the casserole and pour in a strong, well-seasoned broth to cover. Bake, covered, in the preheated oven for 1 hour, or until the rice is thoroughly cooked and the liquid is entirely cooked away. If the broth cooks away before the rice is soft, add a little more to the casserole.

Serves four to six.

Italian Casserole of Chicken

An old Italian cook taught me this dish. She had created it in an emergency, and it was so successful that she kept it in her repertoire and wove a beautiful story around it: "An old Tuscan dish handed down through generations," she said.

1 roasting chicken, 4 pounds
    (1¾ kg)
Celery leaves
3 carrots
1 sprig parsley
2 teaspoons salt
Boiling water to cover
¼ pound (115 g) bacon,
    cut in slivers
2 medium onions, finely
    chopped
2 cloves garlic, finely
    chopped
¼ teaspoon dried thyme
¼ cup (½ dL) olive oil
½ cup (115 g) black
    Italian or Greek
    olives, pitted

1 green pepper, seeded and
    cut into julienne
2 tablespoons (30 g)
    butter
6 large tomatoes, peeled
    and quartered
1 tablespoon chopped fresh
    basil or 1 teaspoon
    dried
Salt and freshly ground
    black pepper to taste
1 pound (450 g) spaghetti
3 tablespoons chopped
    parsley
3 eggs
2/3 cup (60 g) freshly
    grated Parmesan
    cheese

Place the chicken in a kettle with some celery leaves, the carrots, parsley sprig, and 2 teaspoons salt. Cover with boiling water and simmer till tender, about 1 hour. Remove from the broth and allow to cool slightly. Strip all the meat from the bones, cutting the larger pieces into small chunks. Place in a large heatproof casserole.

Cook the bacon in a skillet over a low heat until crisp. Remove and add to the casserole. Sauté the onion, garlic, and thyme in the bacon fat till the onion is transparent but not browned. Add to the casserole.

Heat the olive oil in a clean skillet and sauté the olives and green pepper for 3 to 4 minutes. Add salt to taste and add to the casserole.

Finally, melt the butter in a skillet, add the tomatoes and basil, and cook till well blended but not mushy. Salt and pepper to taste and add to the casserole.

Preheat the oven to 400°F (205°C).

Cook the spaghetti in boiling salted water till *al dente*. This should take from 9 to 12 minutes. Drain and toss with all ingredients in the casserole. Add the chopped parsley.

Beat the eggs till lemon colored and add the grated cheese to make a thick paste. Spread carefully over the spaghetti mixture. Bake in the preheated oven till the eggs and cheese are set and browned. Serve with hot French or Italian bread, which has been split and spread with a mixture of butter, chopped chives, parsley, and a whiff of garlic; a large green salad; and plenty of good claret.

Serves eight to ten.

Old-Fashioned Chicken Casserole

1 roasting chicken, 4 to 5
    pounds (1¾ to 2¼
    kg), cut up
6 tablespoons (85 g) butter
3 medium carrots, scraped
    and cut into julienne
1 stalk celery, trimmed and
    cut into julienne
12 small white onions,
    peeled

1 cup (¼ L) chicken broth
½ teaspoon thyme
Salt and freshly ground
    black pepper to taste
2 cups (½ L) thick
    béchamel sauce (page
    179)
Lemon juice to taste
1 package (10 ounces, 285
    g) frozen small peas

Preheat the oven to 350°F (175°C).

Melt the butter in a skillet and brown the pieces quickly on all sides. Transfer to a 4-quart (4 L) casserole with a cover.

Add the carrots, celery, onions, broth, thyme, and salt and pepper to the casserole. Cover, place in the preheated oven, and cook for about 1½ hours.

Prepare 2 cups of thick béchamel sauce. After the casserole has been in oven for about 1 hour, pour the béchamel over the chicken and vegetable mixture, cover it again, and continue cooking for 30 to 35 minutes, or until the chicken is tender.

Cook the peas according to directions on the package. Add to the casserole, and stir in the lemon juice just as you send it to the table.

Tiny new potatoes are perfect with this dish; or serve rice. Serves six.

Casserole of Chicken with White Wine

1 roasting chicken, 4 pounds
 (1¾ kg)
½ lemon
Stuffing of your choice (see
 pages 169–175)
5 tablespoons olive oil,
 butter, or bacon fat
1 cup (¼ L) white wine, or
 as needed
12 small white onions,
 peeled and sliced

15 small new potatoes,
 peeled and sliced
Salt and freshly ground
 black pepper
12 mushrooms, cleaned and
 halved or quartered,
 if large
Parsley

Preheat the oven to 325°F (165°C).

Rub the inside of the chicken with half a lemon. Stuff and truss the chicken (see page 38). Brown well in a skillet in olive oil, butter, or bacon fat. Place in a flameproof casserole with ½ cup (1 dL) white wine. Cover and bake in the preheated oven for 45 minutes.

In the meantime, sauté the onions and potatoes in the fat remaining in the pan in which you browned the chicken, until nicely browned and partially cooked. Season with salt and pepper to taste.

Remove the casserole from the oven and add the potatoes, onions, mushrooms, and parsley sprig. Salt and pepper the chicken and add remaining wine, then cover and replace in the oven. Cook for another hour, or until the chicken is tender. Serve with the degreased pan juices, slightly thickened if you like, and garnish with the onions, potatoes, and mushrooms. Serves four to six.

Chicken Casserole with Lentils

2 cups (450 g) lentils
1 onion, stuck with 2 cloves
1 bay leaf
1 teaspoon salt
1 roasting chicken, 4 pounds
   (1¾ kg), cut up

Flour for dredging
Salt and freshly ground
   black pepper
5 tablespoons (70 g) butter
Boiling water or broth, if
   needed

Prepare the lentils. Presoak unprocessed lentils for several hours, then drain and place in a kettle with water to cover, an onion stuck with 2 cloves, a bay leaf, and a teaspoon of salt. Bring to a boil, reduce the heat, and simmer until tender. (Quick-cooking lentils require no soaking, and will cook in 25 to 30 minutes.)

Preheat the oven to 350°F (175°C).

Dredge the chicken with flour, salt, and pepper. Heat the butter in a heavy skillet and brown the chicken very quickly. Transfer to a casserole. Add the lentils and the broth in which they were cooked. If there is not enough liquid to cover, add boiling water or broth. Place in the preheated oven and cook slowly for 1½ hours, adding more liquid if necessary.

Serves six.

VARIATION

For a more distinctive flavor, add to the casserole 6 or 7 slices of cotechino or other highly flavored pork sausage, such as the hot Italian variety.

Chicken Tetrazzini

3 cups (340 g) diced,
   cooked chicken
2 cups (½ L) sauce
   suprême (page 179)
1/3 cup (¾ dL) sherry
2 tablespoons chopped
   pimiento (optional)

Salt and freshly ground
   black pepper
12 ounces (335 g) spaghetti
Buttered bread crumbs
Freshly grated Parmesan
   cheese

Heat the diced chicken in the sauce suprême. When it is thoroughly blended and heated through, add the dry sherry and pimiento. Season to taste.

Preheat the oven to 425°F (220°C).

Cook spaghetti in boiling, salted water till it is as tender as you like it. Drain and place in a buttered casserole or baking dish. Cover with the chicken mixture, then sprinkle with buttered crumbs and grated Parmesan cheese and bake in the preheated oven until the top has lightly browned.

Serves six to eight.

Chicken with Forty Cloves of Garlic

8 chicken legs with thighs
40 cloves garlic
4 stalks celery
2/3 cup (1 1/2 dL) olive oil
6 sprigs parsley
1 tablespoon chopped fresh tarragon or 1 1/2 teaspoons dried

1/2 cup (1 dL) dry vermouth
2 1/2 teaspoons salt
1/4 teaspoon fresh ground black pepper
Pinch of freshly grated nutmeg

Preheat the oven to 375°F (190°C).

Wash the chicken legs and thighs and thoroughly dry. Peel the garlic, leaving the cloves whole. Trim the celery, then cut in thin slices. Put the oil in a shallow dish or a plate and turn the chicken in the oil to coat on all sides. Reserve the unused oil. Lay the celery slices in the bottom of a heavy casserole with a tight-fitting cover. Add the parsley and tarragon, then lay the chicken pieces on top. Pour the vermouth over the chicken, and add 1 teaspoon salt, the pepper, and nutmeg.

Pour the reserved oil into the casserole, then toss in all the garlic and sprinkle with the remaining salt. Put a piece of aluminum foil over the casserole and then cover to make a tight seal; or make a thick, heavy flour and water paste to seal the lid, and cover lid and paste with another layer of foil. Bake in the preheated oven for 1 1/2 hours without removing the lid.

Serve with hot toast or thin slices of pumpernickel—to be spread with the garlic sauce. You will find that the garlic has been tamed in the cooking and acquired a delicious buttery quality.

Serves six to eight.

CREAMED CHICKEN

Creamed chicken has become a cliché in the American kitchen and is looked upon by sophisticated cooks with some condescension. However, it can be a pleasant dish, and even a dish of distinction, if the chicken is of good quality and the sauce is prepared with care.

Creamed Chicken

1½ cups (3½ dL) béchamel sauce (page 179)
2 cups (225 g) diced, cooked chicken
2 tablespoons Madeira, sherry, Cognac, or bourbon

4 slices toast, muffins, or patty shells; or boiled rice
1 tablespoon chopped parsley

Prepare the béchamel sauce, and when thickened add the Madeira or other flavoring. Combine with diced chicken in the upper part of a double boiler. Place over simmering water, cover, and allow to heat for 8 to 10 minutes, or until the chicken is blended with sauce and thoroughly heated. Add the chopped parsley. Serve on toast or muffins, in patty shells or on rice.
  Serves four.

Creamed Chicken and Mushrooms

½ pound (225 g) mushrooms, cleaned
1½ cups (3½ dL) water
Salt to taste
2 tablespoons (30 g) butter
2 cups (225 g) diced, cooked chicken

2 cups (½ L) béchamel sauce (page 179)
2 egg yolks
Freshly ground black pepper
Lemon juice to taste

Remove the stems from the mushrooms and slice caps. Chop the stems and simmer in the water for 30 to 40 minutes. Drain off the broth, add salt to taste, and reserve. Lightly sauté the sliced mushrooms in the butter.

Heat the chicken in the béchamel sauce in a double boiler and add the sliced mushrooms and about half the broth. Mix well and remove from the heat. Allow to cool slightly before adding the egg yolks mixed with the remaining broth. Return to low heat and stir till well blended and smooth. Taste for seasoning and squeeze in a few drops of lemon juice.

Serves six.

Chicken à la King

In its day—the 1920s and 1930s—this dish was considered a classic.

3 cups (340 g) diced, cooked chicken
3 tablespoons chopped pimiento or roasted peppers
3 cups (¾ L) sauce suprême (page 179)
6 tablespoons sherry
1 cup (60 g) sliced mushrooms, sautéed in 4 tablespoons (60 g) butter

1 tablespoon chopped green pepper
1 tablespoon grated onion
3 tablespoons chopped parsley
Salt and freshly ground black pepper to taste
Lemon juice to taste

Heat the chicken and pimiento or roasted peppers in the sauce, and add the sherry. Add the sautéed mushrooms, green pepper, onion, parsley, and seasonings.

Serves six.

Creamed Chicken in Noodle Ring

8 ounces (225 g) noodles
4 eggs, separated
1 cup (¼ L) milk or light cream
Salt and freshly ground black pepper to taste

Chicken à la king (see above)
Strips of pimiento or broiled mushroom caps for garnish

Preheat the oven to 350°F (175°C).

Cook the noodles in boiling, salted water till *al dente*, about
9 minutes. Drain. Beat the egg yolks till lemon colored. Add the
milk or light cream, salt, and pepper. Combine with the noodles.
Beat the egg whites until very stiff and fold into the noodle
mixture. Turn into a well-greased 6-cup (1½ L) ring mold.
Place the mold in a pan of hot water and bake in the preheated
oven for 50 to 60 minutes. Unmold on a platter. Fill with hot
chicken à la king and garnish with strips of pimiento or broiled
mushroom caps.

Serves six.

Creamed Chicken with Clams

1½ cups (170 g) diced,
    cooked chicken
2 cups (½ L) velouté sauce
    (page 179), made
    with 1 cup (¼ L)
    clam broth
1 cup (250 g) raw small
    whole clams or minced
    razor clams

3 tablespoons cream
Salt and freshly ground
    black pepper
1 tablespoon chopped
    parsley

Heat the chicken and sauce in a double boiler. Add the clams
and cook gently for a few minutes more or until the clams are
heated through. Stir in the cream, taste for seasoning, and add
the parsley.

Serves four.

VARIATION

With oysters: Proceed as above, substituting oyster liquor in the
velouté sauce and 1 cup (250 g) raw oysters in the chicken
mixture. Heat till the edges of the oysters curl.

Swiss Enchiladas

This Mexican dish is mild in seasoning, delicious, and agreeable
to almost everyone. It is called "Swiss" because of the cream,
which is true of all such dishes in Mexico.

1 onion, chopped
Cooking oil
1 clove garlic, crushed
2 cups (½ L) tomato purée
2 green chilies, chopped
2 cups (225 g) chopped,
    cooked chicken
Salt
1 dozen tortillas

3 cups (¾ L) heavy cream
½ cup (1 dL) concentrated
    chicken stock
½ pound (225 g) jack
    cheese, sliced or grated
Garnish: sliced avocado,
    sliced hard-boiled eggs,
    or green or ripe olives

Preheat the oven to 350°F (175°C).

Prepare the stuffing. Sauté the onion in 2 tablespoons oil until
soft. Then add the garlic, tomato purée, chilies, and chicken.
Add salt to taste and simmer for about 10 minutes. Briefly heat
the tortillas, one at a time, in about 1 inch hot oil. Do not let
them get crisp, as they are to be rolled.

Heat the cream, and add the chicken stock. Dip each tortilla
into the cream mixture, place a generous portion of chicken
filling on it, and roll it up. Arrange the rolls in a baking pan,
seam side down, and pour the remaining cream mixture over
them. Top with the jack cheese and bake in the preheated oven
for about 30 minutes.

Garnish with avocado, hard-boiled eggs, or olives.
Serves six.

Chicken Crêpes

3 cups (340 g) chopped,
    cooked chicken
2 cups (½ L) sauce
    suprême (page 179),
    flavored with 2 table-
    spoons Madeira

2 tablespoons finely
    chopped parsley
12 to 14 crêpes (see below)
Freshly grated Parmesan
    cheese

Mix the chicken, two-thirds of the sauce, and chopped parsley.
Place a generous spoonful down the center of each crêpe, and
roll. Arrange, seam side down, in a buttered 9 x 14-inch (23 x
36 cm) baking dish. Spoon the remaining sauce over the crêpes
and sprinkle lightly with cheese. Bake in a 375°F (190°C)
oven till heated through and the cheese is lightly browned.

Serves six.

Basic Crêpes

1 cup minus 2 tablespoons
(125 g) flour
3 eggs
4 to 5 tablespoons melted
butter

⅛ teaspoon salt
1 to 1¼ cups (¼ L to 3½
dL) milk, or as
needed

The crêpe batter can be made in an electric blender, food processor, or mixer; or in a bowl, using a rotary beater, hand electric beater, or wire whisk. First mix the flour, eggs, butter, and salt. Then gradually add milk until the batter has the consistency of light cream. Let the batter rest for 2 hours before using.

To make crêpes, butter a 6-inch (15-cm) pan with rounded sides, a crêpe pan if possible. Place the pan over medium-high heat. When the butter sizzles, pour a little batter into the pan, tilting and rotating so the batter coats the surface evenly. Pour any excess batter back into the bowl. Cook each crêpe until lightly browned on the underside, then turn and brown the other side. Remove from the pan and keep warm, covered with foil, until ready to use.

Breasts of Chicken Suprême

2 whole chicken breasts, cut
in half, boned, and
skinned
4 tablespoons (60 g) butter
Salt and freshly ground
black pepper
1 to 1½ cups (85 g)
buttered bread crumbs,
as needed

4 slices baked ham
12 mushroom caps of uniform size
2 cups sauce suprême (page
179)
¼ cup (½ dL) sherry
Chopped parsley

Trim the chicken fillets nicely so they look neat and are of an even size. Sauté them gently in the butter till just cooked and lightly browned. Season with salt and pepper to taste, and roll in buttered crumbs.

Trim the ham slices so they are roughly the size of the fillets. Frizzle in the sauté pan just long enough to heat them through.

Brush the mushroom caps with butter and broil until lightly browned.

Prepare the sauce suprême, stir in the sherry, and heat for a few moments more. Arrange the ham slices on a hot platter. Place a chicken fillet on each slice. Spoon the sauce over the fillets and top with mushrooms. Sprinkle with chopped parsley. Serves four.

VARIATION
Arrange the sautéed fillets in a baking dish, top with sauce, sprinkle with buttered crumbs, grated Parmesan cheese, and paprika and brown quickly in a 350°F (175°C) oven.

Hot Chicken Salad

This is an admirable way to use leftover chicken, especially dark meat if you have served the breast of chicken the day before.

2 cups (225 g) diced, cooked chicken
½ cup (60 g) finely cut celery
2 tablespoons grated onion
2 tablespoons chopped parsley
Salt and freshly ground black pepper

Lemon juice to taste
1 cup (¼ L) béchamel sauce (page 179)
1 cup (¼ L) tart mayonnaise
Paprika
¼ cup (30 g) sliced almonds, toasted

Preheat the oven to 350°F (175°C).

Mix the chicken, celery, onion, and parsley. Season to taste with salt and pepper and a few drops of lemon juice. Prepare the béchamel sauce, and after it has cooled slightly, fold in the tart mayonnaise, made by whipping in an extra amount of lemon juice. Taste for seasoning, for this should have a decidedly tart flavor. You may need to add a few more drops of lemon juice. Arrange the chicken mixture in individual baking dishes or ramekins and top with the sauce. Dust with paprika and bake in the preheated oven for 10 to 15 minutes; the chicken should be heated through. Top with almonds and serve with peas and watermelon pickle.
Serves four.

VARIATION

You may add 1 tablespoon chopped green pepper or pimiento or 1 tablespoon finely cut sweet pickle to the chicken mixture for a different flavor.

Creamed Chicken with Eggs

This recipe is sometimes called Chicken Terrapin.

3 cups (340 g) diced, cooked chicken

2 cups (½ L) béchamel sauce (page 179), flavored with ¼ cup (½ dL) sherry

3 hard-boiled eggs, yolks and whites separated and chopped

Salt and freshly ground black pepper

6 slices toast

Chopped parsley

Heat the chicken in the top of a double boiler with the béchamel sauce flavored with sherry. Add the chopped egg yolks. Blend well, taste for seasoning, and serve on toast garnished with the chopped egg whites and parsley.

Serves six.

CHICKEN PIES

French Chicken Pie

6 to 8 chicken legs and thighs, according to size

Flour for dredging

6 tablespoons (85 g) butter

4 hard-boiled eggs, shelled and halved

3 to 4 slices bacon, cut in small pieces

2 onions, finely chopped

1 clove garlic, crushed

1 bay leaf

1 teaspoon dried thyme

½ pound (225 g) mushrooms, sliced

¼ cup (½ dL) white wine

Salt and freshly ground black pepper to taste

Pastry of your choice for 1 crust

1 egg, beaten with 1 tablespoon cream

Dust the chicken pieces lightly with flour and brown on all sides in butter in a sauté pan. Arrange in a round baking dish with the hard-boiled eggs. Add the bacon, onion, garlic, and herbs to the sauté pan. Cook until the onion is just soft, then add the mushrooms and wine. Season with salt and pepper, cover, and simmer for 45 minutes. Pour the mixture in the pan over the chicken; allow to cool.

Roll out the pastry to fit the top of the dish. Cut a vent in the middle and place a small funnel of waxed paper in it to let the steam escape. Brush the pastry with the egg-cream mixture and bake in a 375°F (190°C) oven for 25 to 30 minutes, or until the crust is thoroughly cooked.

To serve, cut a wedge of crust and set aside. Extract a leg and half an egg and put them on a warm plate. Spoon some of the bacon, mushrooms, and juices over them, and top with the wedge of crust.

Serves six.

Pennsylvania Chicken Pie

1 chicken, 3 pounds
     (1350 g)
½ lemon
Boiling, salted water to
     cover
1 medium onion, stuck with
     3 cloves
Celery leaves
12 small white onions,
     peeled
6 carrots, scraped and
     quartered
16 potato balls or very
     small new potatoes,
     peeled
Salt and freshly ground
     black pepper
Chopped parsley
Pinch of dried marjoram
Béchamel sauce (page
     179), using 1 cup
     combined chicken and
     vegetable broth
Rich pastry of your choice
     for 1 crust

Rub the inside of the chicken with half a lemon. Place in a pot and cover with salted, boiling water. Add the onion stuck with the cloves and a few celery leaves, cover loosely, and simmer until tender. Cool in the broth. Strip the meat from the bones and cut into small chunks; reserve the broth.

In a separate pan, cook the small onions, carrots, and potatoes in water to cover until tender. Drain, saving the broth, and season with salt and pepper to taste.

Preheat the oven to 450°F (230°C).

Arrange the chicken and vegetables in an ovenproof casserole or baking dish. Season with salt and pepper, and sprinkle with chopped parsley and a pinch of marjoram. Make the béchamel sauce, using 1 cup of combined chicken and vegetable broth, and pour over the chicken. Cool. Cover with rich pastry and bake in the preheated oven for 10 minutes. Reduce the heat to 375°F (190°C) and continue baking till the pastry is cooked, about 30 minutes.

Serves six.

Old-Fashioned Chicken Pie

1 roasting chicken, 5 pounds (2¼ kg), cut up, or an equivalent amount of chicken parts
1 medium onion
Celery leaves
1 bay leaf
Water to cover
Salt and freshly ground black pepper
12 small white onions, peeled
4 carrots, scraped and quartered
3 tablespoons flour
3 tablespoons (45 g) butter
1 cup (¼ L) light cream or half and half
Pinch of freshly ground nutmeg
Chopped parsley
Paprika
Biscuit crust or flaky pastry of your choice

Place the chicken in a kettle with the onion, a few celery leaves, bay leaf, and water to cover. Cover tightly and simmer till tender, about 45 minutes. Salt and pepper the broth to taste.

In a separate pan, cook the white onions and carrots in water to cover till just tender. Drain and add salt to taste. Prepare a sauce by blending the flour and butter in a saucepan over low heat. Add 2 cups (½ L) of the chicken broth and stir till thickened. Add the light cream and blend well. Season to taste with salt and a pinch of nutmeg.

Arrange the chicken and vegetables in a baking dish. Pile

higher in the center of the dish or place an ovenproof egg cup or regular cup in the center to hold up the crust. Cover with the sauce and sprinkle with chopped parsley and paprika. Cool. Top with a biscuit crust or pastry, as you wish. Make a large vent in the crust to permit the steam to escape, or insert a funnel of brown paper or foil. For biscuit crust, bake in a 425°F (220°C) oven for 20 to 25 minutes. For pastry, bake at 450°F (230°C) for 10 minutes, then reduce the heat to 375°F (190°C) and continue baking till the pastry is cooked.

Cole slaw is a natural with this dish.

Serves six to eight.

Special Chicken Pie

Rich pastry of your choice
for 2 crusts, rolled
very thin
3 whole chicken breasts, cut
in half, skinned, and
boned
4 tablespoons (60 g) butter
1 cup (60 g) sliced mush-
rooms, sautéed in
butter

2 tablespoons chopped
parsley
2½ cups (6 dL) sauce
suprême (page 179),
flavored with 3 table-
spoons Cognac
1 cup (115 g) sliced
almonds, blanched

Preheat the oven to 450°F (230°C).

Line an 11 x 14-inch (28 x 36 cm) oblong pan or baking dish with half the thinly rolled rich pastry. Cut the remaining pastry into strips and reserve. Separate each chicken fillet into 2 pieces and pound between sheets of waxed paper or foil. Sauté for a few seconds on each side in the butter to merely color. Arrange in the baking dish. Add the sautéed mushrooms and chopped parsley. Pour over this the sauce suprême flavored with the Cognac. Arrange the reserved strips of pastry over the pan in lattice fashion. Sprinkle with the almonds. Bake in the pre-heated 450°F (230°C) oven for 10 minutes, then reduce the heat to 375°F (190°C) and continue cooking till the pastry is crisp and brown. Cut in squares and serve.

Serves six.

CHICKEN SALADS

Chicken Mayonnaise

This is the father and mother of all chicken salads and used to be a standard supper dish for summer.

Cut cold roasted or poached chicken in convenient portions for serving, and remove all the skin. Roll each piece in well-flavored mayonnaise to coat thoroughly. Arrange on a platter and garnish with sliced hard-boiled eggs, stuffed olives, and capers. Dust with chopped parsley. Surround the dish with tomato wedges and sliced cucumbers.

This dish is equally good made with cold duck or turkey.

Simple Chicken Salad

Cut up the meat of a cold chicken in generous-sized cubes. Blend with a well-flavored homemade olive oil mayonnaise (page 181). Arrange on crisp leaves of romaine and garnish with sliced blanched almonds and chopped parsley. That's all there is to it.

Traditional Chicken Salad

The basic proportions of this salad are 2 cups (225 g) diced, cooked chicken to 1 cup (115 g) finely cut celery. Season with salt and freshly ground black pepper to taste and bind with mayonnaise. To serve traditionally, decorate with mayonnaise, sliced hard-boiled eggs, and capers.

Four cups (450 g) of chicken salad will serve five people. If you are going into quantity feeding—a large supper party, for instance—you may stretch it a bit with more celery.

Thus, for 25 people you will want 3 quarts (1350 g) of diced chicken and 1½ quarts (690 g) diced celery. For 50 people you will want 6 quarts (2¾ kg) chicken to 3 quarts (1350 g) celery.

VARIATIONS

Add to 2 cups (225 g) diced cooked chicken:

1. 1½ cups (170 g) cooked green beans marinated in a

vinaigrette dressing. Mix with the chicken. Top with mayonnaise and decorate with tomato quarters.

2. ½ cup (60 g) celery, ½ cup (60 g) sliced ripe olives, ½ cup (60 g) shaved toasted almonds. Bind with mayonnaise and decorate with almonds and olives.

3. 1 cup (115 g) cold cooked green peas marinated in vinaigrette dressing. Bind with mayonnaise and decorate with raw peas.

4. 1 cup (115 g) lightly toasted English walnut meats. Bind with mayonnaise and decorate with pimiento strips.

5. 1 cup (200 g) coarsely chopped hard-boiled eggs, 2 tablespoons chopped sweet pickle, 2 tablespoons chopped parsley. Bind with mayonnaise.

6. 1 cup (115 g) diced cooked sweetbreads, ½ cup (60 g) diced cucumbers. Bind with mayonnaise and decorate with sliced cucumbers.

7. 1 cup (115 g) seedless white grapes, ½ cup (60 g) sliced almonds. Bind with mayonnaise and decorate with preserved kumquats.

8. 1 cup (115 g) diced avocado. Dress with Russian dressing and decorate with ripe olives.

9. 1 cup (115 g) finely cut celery. Bind with mayonnaise and decorate with asparagus tips. Use 4 to 6 tips for each person.

10. 1½ cups (115 g) cold cooked rice marinated in 1 cup (¼ L) vinaigrette dressing and 1 tablespoon grated onion, 1 tablespoon chopped chives, 2 tablespoons chopped parsley, 2 tablespoons chopped green pepper, 1 tablespoon chopped pimiento and ½ cup (115 g) chopped ripe olives. Dress with additional vinaigrette dressing.

CHICKEN SANDWICHES

My Favorite Chicken Sandwich

Take thin slices of good white bread—homemade, if you have it—otherwise a home-style bread. Butter them well, place a generous supply of thinly sliced chicken on the slices, and sprinkle with salt. Press the slices together. Mayonnaise may be added if you like.

For luncheon sandwiches, use slices of bread ¼ inch (¾ cm) thick. For tea and cocktail sandwiches, the bread should be so thin it resembles lace. Cut sandwiches into neat squares or fingers and let them chill, covered with a damp tea towel or cheesecloth, in the refrigerator for an hour or two before serving.

Club House Sandwich

It may seem superfluous to include this veteran, but it is so often badly or incorrectly made that it could stand reviewing.

FOR EACH SANDWICH

2 slices crisp, hot buttered
    toast
3 or 4 slices crisp, hot bacon
4 slices peeled ripe tomato

Chicken slices, as many as
    you want
Mayonnaise
Lettuce (optional)

Construct in this order: toast, chicken, tomato, mayonnaise, bacon, lettuce, toast. The mayonnaise then holds the bacon and prevents slipping and sliding. Green olives and sweet pickles are the traditional accompaniments.

To serve at a large party have the toasters going, arrange plates of the other makings, and let everyone do his or her own construction work.

Composed Sandwich

This sandwich makes a wonderful meal. One of its variations is the stalwart Reuben sandwich. Here is the basic recipe.

2 large slices Russian rye
    bread or pumpernickel,
    well buttered
3 or 4 thick slices of chicken
    or turkey
3 thin slices Swiss cheese

2 slices baked Virginia ham
    or smoked tongue
3 slices tomato
4 thin slices dill pickle
Russian dressing

VARIATIONS
1. Add cole slaw and Bermuda onion.
2. Use sliced American cheese instead of Swiss.
3. Add crisp bacon slices.
4. Add sauerkraut.

Toasted Chicken Sandwich

Remove the crusts from crisp hot toast. Butter well and quickly add thin slices of chicken. A little mayonnaise is acceptable here. Sweet pickles, too, seem to have an affection for toasted chicken sandwiches.

Chicken Salad Sandwich

Choose among the chicken salads given on pages 65–66 to use as a filling. Spread on buttered slices of bread. Naturally, the quality of the sandwich will depend on the quality of the bread. Use homemade, if possible. This sandwich is especially good on thin slices of buttered rye.

CHICKEN HASH, CROQUETTES, SOUFFLÉS

Superb Chicken Hash

1 large onion, finely chopped

2 green peppers, seeded and diced

5 tablespoons (70 g) butter

2 tablespoons cooking oil

4 cups (450 g) or more diced, cooked chicken

Salt and freshly ground black pepper to taste

Tabasco to taste

1 ½ teaspoons dried tarragon

½ cup (30 g) chopped parsley

½ cup (60 g) blanched almonds or broken walnut meats

8 eggs, lightly beaten

¾ cup (70 g) freshly grated Parmesan cheese

Sauté the onion and green pepper in the butter and oil until just wilted. Add the chicken and mix well. Add the seasonings, herbs, and almonds, and toss. Press the chicken down well in the skillet, cover, and cook over medium heat for 2 or 3 minutes. When the chicken is heated through, pour in the beaten eggs mixed with the cheese and cook over low heat until set. If practicable, place under the broiler for 2 or 3 minutes to brown.

Serves six.

Simple Chicken Hash

2 to 3 cups (225–340 g)
    pieces of leftover
    chicken
Stuffing (if available)
1 medium onion, chopped
    very fine
4 tablespoons (60 g) butter
    or bacon fat

2 tablespoons chopped
    parsley
Salt and freshly ground
    black pepper
Freshly grated nutmeg to
    taste
½ cup (1 dL) heavy cream

Cut the chicken into small dice or chop coarsely. If there is any stuffing left, add up to 1 cup to the chicken and blend well. Sauté the onion in the butter or fat. Add the chicken, stuffing, and parsley and mix thoroughly. Season with salt and pepper to taste and add a few grains of nutmeg. Pour in the cream and let it cook down till the hash has formed a pleasant brown crust at the bottom of the pan. Fold over with a spatula and serve with a green salad and some watermelon pickles. This recipe can also be made with leftover turkey.

Serves four to six.

Chicken Hash in Cream

This recipe may also be used as a filling for crêpes.

4 tablespoons (60 g) butter
2 cups (225 g) diced,
    cooked chicken
2 tablespoons chopped
    parsley
2 tablespoons grated onion

Salt and freshly ground
    black pepper
1 cup (¼ L) light
    béchamel sauce (page
    179)
Buttered bread crumbs

Melt the butter in a heavy-bottomed skillet over a low flame. Add the chicken, parsley, and onion and toss well in the pan. Season with salt and pepper to taste and simmer till the chicken is thoroughly heated and slightly browned. Add the béchamel sauce and let simmer for 5 minutes. Sprinkle with buttered crumbs and serve with hot cornbread.

Serves four.

Chicken Croquettes

2 cups (225 g) finely
  chopped, cooked
  chicken
1 tablespoon chopped
  parsley
Salt and freshly ground
  black pepper
Pinch of freshly grated
  nutmeg

1 cup (¼ L) thick
  béchamel sauce (page
  179)
Flour for dredging
2 eggs, lightly beaten
1 cup (60 g) finely grated
  fresh bread crumbs, or
  as needed
Fat for deep frying

Combine the chicken, parsley, and seasonings with the béchamel sauce. Allow to cool. Refrigerate for 2 to 3 hours.

With floured hands, shape the chilled chicken mixture into 10 or 12 balls or rolls. Dip in flour, then in beaten egg, and then in crumbs. Fry for approximately 3 minutes in deep fat, a few at a time, at a temperature of 370°F (185°C). Serve with sauce suprême (page 179).

VARIATIONS

1. Substitute 1 cup (60 g) finely chopped raw mushrooms for 1 cup (115 g) of the chicken.
2. Add 1 tablespoon grated onion and 1 teaspoon chopped fresh tarragon to the mixture.
3. Substitute ½ cup (60 g) chopped almonds or walnuts for ½ cup (60 g) of the chicken.

Chicken Soufflé

4 tablespoons (60 g) butter
¼ cup (35 g) flour
1½ cups (3½ dL) milk or
  chicken stock
2 cups (225 g) finely
  ground, cooked chicken

Salt and freshly ground
  black pepper
Pinch of freshly grated
  nutmeg
6 eggs, separated

Preheat the oven to 350°F (175°C).

Make a thick béchamel sauce using the butter, flour and milk (see page 179). When thickened, add the finely ground chicken, salt and pepper to taste, and nutmeg. Cool slightly, then add the egg yolks, beaten. Heat over hot, not boiling, water till the mixture is thickened. Cool again. Beat the egg whites stiff and fold in; pour the mixture into a buttered 2-quart (2 L) soufflé dish. Bake in a pan of hot water in the preheated oven for 30 to 40 minutes, till puffed and brown. Serve at once.

Serves four.

VARIATIONS
1. Substitute 1 cup (60 g) mushrooms, finely chopped and sautéed, for 1 cup (115 g) of the chicken.
2. Add 3 tablespoons sherry to the sauce.

CHICKEN GIBLETS

Chicken Livers en Brochette

Clean chicken livers and separate each into 2 pieces. Roll in thin slices of partially cooked bacon and secure on metal skewers, allowing 4 or 5 livers to a serving. Broil under a low flame till the bacon is crisp, turning the skewers frequently so the bacon is evenly cooked. Serve on a bed of parsley.

These also make a good accompaniment to drinks, in which case fasten each piece of liver and bacon with toothpicks or small bamboo skewers.

VARIATION
Marinate the livers in soy sauce, chopped garlic, and grated fresh ginger before wrapping in bacon.

Sauté of Chicken Livers

3 or 4 shallots, finely chopped
4 tablespoons (60 g) butter
1 pound (450 g) chicken livers, cleaned and separated into 2 pieces each

2 tablespoons chopped parsley
Salt and freshly ground black pepper
4 slices crisp toast

Sauté the shallots for 3 or 4 minutes in the butter. Add the chicken livers and sauté gently till nicely browned and cooked through. Add the chopped parsley and salt and pepper to taste. Serve on crisp toast.

Serves four.

VARIATIONS

1. These sautéed livers may be folded into an omelet for four.
2. Serve on a bed of buttered and well-flavored noodles, and add a bit of nutmeg as well as salt and pepper.

Giblet Sauté

½ pound (225 g) chicken gizzards

3 or 4 chicken hearts, coarsely chopped

½ pound (225 g) chicken livers, cut in 2 pieces each

5 tablespoons (70 g) butter

1 tablespoon grated onion

2 tablespoons chopped parsley

1 tablespoon chopped chives

Salt and freshly ground black pepper

Simmer the gizzards and hearts for 25 minutes in boiling water. Drain. Melt 4 tablespoons (60 g) of the butter in a skillet. Add the gizzards, cut into halves or quarters, hearts, and livers. Cook over a low flame, tossing well, till browned and well blended. Add the onion, parsley, and chives, season with salt and pepper to taste and add the remaining butter. Increase the heat to moderate and cook for 2 minutes, stirring well. Serve over rice or well-buttered noodles.

Serves four.

VARIATION

Chopped Giblet Sandwich: Sauté the gizzards, hearts, and livers in butter as directed above. Chop medium fine in a wooden chopping bowl and add more chopped parsley and a bit more onion if desired. Add a dash of Tabasco. Spread on slices of well-buttered toast, and top with additional toast.

FRESH CORNISH GAME HEN

Cornish game hen can be prepared in many of the ways suggested for chicken but is especially good roasted or sautéed. However, I recommend using only fresh birds, which at present are limited in distribution to the New York metropolitan area and come from Perdue Farms in Maryland. These young hens, five to six weeks old, range from 1 to 1¾ pounds (450–800 g) and are delicate in flavor and tender. They are also far less expensive than domestic game birds like quail and partridge. Plan to serve one game hen per person.

Roast Cornish Game Hen

Rub inside and out with half a lemon, brush well with oil, and season with salt and pepper (or use one of the treatments suggested for roast chicken), and roast in a 425°F (220°C) oven for 22 minutes, brushing with additional oil after 10 minutes. Don't be afraid to use your fingers to eat these delicious birds.

Roast Stuffed Cornish Game Hen

1 game hen per person   ½ lemon

FOR EACH BIRD
⅓ cup (40 g) chopped onion or shallot   Melted butter
1 tablespoon (15 g) butter   Salt and pepper
⅔ cup (40 g) fresh bread crumbs   Tarragon, rosemary or thyme—fresh or dried
     Dash of Cognac or Madeira

Rub each bird inside and out with half a lemon. Sauté the chopped onion or shallot in the tablespoon of butter. Add the bread crumbs and enough melted butter to moisten them. Season with salt and pepper, and add your choice of herb and a dash of Cognac or Madeira. Blend all ingredients, and stuff each bird. Skewer the vents or close with a piece of foil, truss (see page 38), and roast on a rack in a 350°F (175°C) oven for 30 to 35 minutes.

Sautéed Cornish Game Hen

Split each bird in half and sauté quickly in butter and oil for about 8 to 10 minutes on each side; or use one of the treatments suggested for sautéed chicken.

Broiled Cornish Game Hen

Split each bird down the back and flatten to provide more even cooking. Brush with oil and season with salt and pepper (or use one of the treatments suggested for broiled chicken) and broil 4 inches under moderate heat about 8 to 10 minutes on each side.

CHICKEN BROTH AND SOUPS

Chicken broth or stock has many uses in the kitchen. It can be served clear or in combination with other ingredients for soup; it forms the basis for many other soups and can be used for sauces and aspics, as an additive to braised dishes, and for cooking certain vegetables. Most good cooks keep a supply of it frozen. For general purposes, use backs, necks, and gizzards rather than other chicken parts or a whole chicken. Not only is this more economical, but it provides good flavor and can be cooked down without regard for the meat.

Basic Chicken Broth

4 pounds (1¾ kg) chicken backs, necks, and gizzards
3 quarts (3 L) water
Celery tops or 1 or 2 stalks celery
1 medium onion, stuck with 2 cloves

1 sprig parsley
1 clove garlic
6 peppercorns
Salt to taste, or about 1 tablespoon

Place the chicken parts and gizzards in a soup kettle and add the water, celery, onion, parsley, garlic, and peppercorns. Bring slowly to a boil and skim off any scum that forms. Reduce the heat, cover, and simmer gently for 2 to 2½ hours. Add salt to taste and strain through a linen cloth or filter paper. Allow to cool, and skim off the fat.

VARIATIONS

1. Combine with an equal amount of tomato juice and a pinch of cayenne pepper. Heat and serve.
2. Cream Soup: Add 2 egg yolks and 1 cup (¼ L) cream, lightly beaten together, for each 4 cups (1 L) of broth. Stir constantly over low heat till the soup is of a desired thickness; do not allow to boil. Season to taste and garnish with bits of shredded chicken and chopped parsley.
3. Noodle Soup: Cook 4 ounces (115 g) of egg noodles with 1 quart (1 L) of broth and add shreds of chicken.
4. Add 1 tablespoon of Madeira or sherry to each cup (¼ L) of soup.

Chicken Consommé

5 to 6 pounds (2¼ to 2¾ kg) chicken backs, necks and gizzards
1 veal knuckle
2 pounds (900 g) shin of beef with bone
1 onion, stuck with 3 cloves
2 to 3 carrots
3 sprigs parsley
2 celery tops or 2 stalks celery
1 clove garlic
¼ teaspoon dried thyme
1 tablespoon salt
1 tablespoon peppercorns
4 quarts (4 L) cold water
3 egg whites

You will need an 8- or 10-quart (8–10 L) kettle for this soup. Combine all the ingredients (except the egg white). Bring to a boil, and skim off any scum that forms. Then turn the heat low and cover so the broth simmers very gently for 4 or 5 hours, adding hot water if there is too much evaporation. Strain off the broth. Let it cool. Then skim off all fat.

To clarify (for 2 to 3 quarts broth): Be sure the pot in which you clarify is spotlessly clean. Pour the broth into the pot. Beat the egg whites to soft peaks and add to the broth. Whisk over medium heat until the broth comes to a boil. Reduce the heat and simmer for 15 minutes, then allow to stand for 10 to 12 minutes. Strain through a linen cloth or several thicknesses of filter paper. (Coffee filters work very well.)

To serve: This may be served clear or with any of the following: egg or spinach noodles; rice; thin slices of soft, ripe avocado added just before serving; a touch of Madeira or sherry; tiny croutons of bread, fried in butter; chopped chives and parsley; tarragon and white wine; chopped hard-boiled egg and paprika; chopped raw spinach; rounds of toasted, buttered bread sprinkled with grated Parmesan cheese.

The broth or consommé may be frozen and used as you need it.

Serves eight.

Crème Vichyssoise

This popular soup was created in New York by the famous chef Louis Diat. The following recipe is my own version. Essentially, this is a leek and potato soup, served cold.

8 to 10 leeks
3 tablespoons (45 g) butter
    or chicken fat
3 cups (¾ L) chicken
    broth, or as needed
4 medium mealy potatoes,
    peeled

Salt and freshly ground
    black pepper to taste
½ teaspoon freshly grated
    nutmeg
1¼ cups (3 dL) sweet or
    sour cream or yogurt,
    or to taste
Chopped chives

Cut the green tops from the leeks and save for flavoring other soups. Cut the white part into 1-inch (2½ cm) lengths and clean thoroughly under cold running water. In butter or chicken fat, sauté the white part of the leeks gently, being careful not to brown. When wilted, add 1 cup (¼ L) chicken broth and simmer gently. Meanwhile, boil the potatoes in salted water.

When the potatoes and leeks are tender, combine them, add another 1 cup (¼ L) chicken broth, and let them simmer together for 10 minutes. Crush the potatoes with a fork so they become saturated with the leek flavor. Season with salt and pepper to taste and add the nutmeg.

Force the vegetables through a fine sieve or food mill with

the broth. Add another 1 cup (¼ L) broth, or more if the vegetable purée seems too thick. When it is cool, place it in the refrigerator and chill it for 18 to 24 hours.

The last step is to add cream, sour cream, or yogurt to the purée. You will need about 1½ cups of cream to each quart of purée (3½ dL per 1 L). But that is really something you will have to work out for your own taste. Be sure that the soup is well chilled when served. Top each serving with chopped chives or pass the chives separately.

Serves six.

VARIATIONS

Curried: Add 1 teaspoon or more, according to your taste, of curry powder to the purée when it is still hot. This is relished by a great many people. You may also use chopped fresh coriander, if you like its flavor, instead of chives.

With cucumber: Peel and split a crisp cucumber. Remove all seeds and cut in rather thin half moons. Fold into the soup an hour or so before serving.

Apple Vichyssoise: Thin shreds or slices of tart apple may be combined with the soup an hour before serving.

A Rich Cream of Chicken Soup

1 chicken, 4 pounds
  (1¾ kg)
2 or 3 leeks
1 onion, stuck with 3 cloves
Celery tops
1 tablespoon peppercorns
Cold water to cover

Salt and finely ground
  black pepper
1½ cups (3½ dL) cream,
  blended with 3 egg
  yolks
2 tablespoons sherry
Blanched almonds
  (optional)

Choose a good plump chicken. Place it in a pot with the leeks, the onion stuck with the cloves, several celery tops, and the peppercorns. Cover with cold water and simmer till tender. Remove the meat from the breast and reserve. Return the carcass with the remaining meat to the broth; simmer another hour.

Remove the carcass. Season the broth to taste, skim off the fat, and strain through cheesecloth.

Strip the meat from the carcass and put through a food processor or chop very fine. Add the chopped meat to the strained broth, heat thoroughly, and add the cream and egg yolks. Do not allow to boil. Stir constantly till the soup is slightly thickened; add the sherry. Cut the breast meat into julienne and add to the soup. Thinly shaved almonds may be used as a garnish. Serves six.

Chicken Mushroom Soup

½ pound (225 g) mush-
    rooms, very thinly
    sliced
3 tablespoons (45 g) butter
3 cups (¾ L) chicken broth

Salt to taste
1 cup (¼ L) hot cream,
    blended with 2 egg
    yolks
3 tablespoons Madeira

Sauté the mushrooms in the butter, reserving a mushroom cap for each serving. When soft but not browned—about 5 minutes —add the chicken broth and simmer gently till heated through. Add salt to taste and the hot cream blended with the egg yolks. Stir constantly over low heat till the soup is slightly thickened; do not allow to boil. Add the Madeira. Garnish each cup with a broiled mushroom cap.

Serves six.

Cold Pea Soup

½ cup (115 g) soaked
    green split peas
3 cups (¾ L) chicken broth
Salt and freshly ground
    black pepper to taste

1 cup (¼ L) heavy cream
    or yogurt
Finely chopped fresh mint

Simmer the soaked split peas in the chicken broth till tender. Force through a fine sieve and season to taste with salt and pepper. Chill for 24 hours and combine with cream or yogurt. Chill again for an hour before serving and serve with finely chopped mint.

Serves four.

2

Turkey

The national holiday bird is now with us the year round and is as readily available in markets as chicken. Like chicken, it is being sold in parts, providing the chance to enjoy turkey for a meal or two without facing a week of leftovers. Turkey breasts are good buys for small families who prefer white meat; and dark meat fanciers can indulge themselves in legs and thighs. In addition, whole turkeys for roasting are produced in a tremendous range of sizes, from 4 or 5 pounds (1¾–2¼ kg) to 30 pounds (13½ kg) and over. Many of these come with fat inserted under the skin for self basting, and others come boned and rolled. While frozen birds dominate, it is still possible to find fresh-killed turkeys throughout the country.

Turkey is being used in more imaginative ways than ever before, but the classic preparation is still that of roasting. Unfortunately there are no definitive rules to guide the inexperienced cook, but after a lifetime of turkey, this is the procedure I now recommend.

Basic Roast Turkey

1 turkey, 18 to 20 pounds
    (8¼–9 kg)
½ lemon
Stuffing of your choice (see
    pages 169–175)
8 tablespoons (115 g) or
    more softened butter

Salt and freshly ground
    black pepper
Strips of fresh siding or
    larding pork, or bacon
    rind

Preheat the oven to 350°F (175°C).

Rub the inside of the turkey with half a lemon, and dry with paper towels. Fill the body and neck cavities with stuffing, but not too tightly—the crumbs should remain somewhat loose. Place a piece of folded foil over the stuffing in the vent, then secure the neck skin and vent with skewers, and truss (see below). Massage the skin well with the softened butter, then salt and pepper it.

Line a roasting rack with strips of siding, larding pork, or bacon rind, which you can sometimes buy from your butcher when he cuts down a whole slab. Set the rack in a fairly shallow roasting pan and place the turkey, breast side down, on the rack. Roast for 1 hour in the preheated oven, then turn the turkey on its side (to turn the bird, I use wads of paper towels), and rub with butter. Roast for another hour. Turn on its other side, and rub with butter. Roast for a third hour. Turn the turkey on its back and rub the breast with butter. Return to the oven and continue roasting till the turkey tests done. Remove from the oven and place on a hot platter. Allow the bird to rest for 15 minutes if being served hot. If being served tepid, let it cool gently at room temperature. Remove all the twine and skewers. Proceed to carve.

Serves sixteen or more.

STUFFING

Stuff both the vent and neck cavity of the bird, using approximately ¾ to 1 cup of stuffing per pound (450 g). Thus, a turkey of 20 pounds (9 kg) will take 15 to 20 cups. Do not pack, but fill loosely. If you like, use one type of stuffing for the vent and another for the neck—for example, a bread stuffing and a sausage stuffing. Draw the neck skin over the stuffing and tie it well or secure with skewers. Sew up the vent or arrange a piece of folded foil over the stuffing and skewer the opening.

TRUSSING

Turn the wing tips under the back of the turkey. Using a long piece of kitchen string, tie the legs together, wrap around the tail, and then secure the legs and tail together, leaving two lengths of string. Cross these under the middle of the back, wrap around each wing, bring together over the breast and tie.

To keep the legs closer to the body, insert a skewer in the joint between each leg and thigh. Tie a piece of string from one skewer to the other, running it under the back.

TESTING

The trick of roasting a turkey is to keep the white meat from becoming dry while cooking the dark meat sufficiently. There is no certain test to tell you when the turkey is done, and you must rely a good bit on your judgment. Here are two general rules to help you. First, see if the leg can be moved up and down *somewhat* flexibly. (To my mind, by the time the leg is really loose, the bird is overdone.) Second, prick the leg joint with a fork: if the juices run clear or faintly pink, the bird is done.

VARIATIONS

With garlic and black pepper: Stuff the turkey with a 6-inch (15 cm) length of dry French bread that has been rubbed with garlic to saturate it, and then rolled in freshly ground black pepper. This makes a fairly heady seasoning, and is especially good for small turkeys roasted on the spit.

Truffled Turkey: Use either the white Italian truffles or the black French variety. The night before roasting the turkey, cut the truffles in slices ⅛ inch (⅓ cm) thick. Loosen the breast skin with your fingers and arrange the truffle slices underneath. Also place several slices in the cavity of the bird if you are not stuffing it. Secure the neck and skin and vent, and truss (see page 82). Rub well with a mixture of salt, freshly ground black pepper, butter, and a little thyme. Follow basic roasting directions above.

TRADITIONAL ACCOMPANIMENTS FOR ROAST TURKEY

Baked ham; grilled pork sausages of various kinds; puréed potatoes and puréed yellow turnips, either separate or mixed; creamed dried corn; roasted chestnuts or chestnut purée; baked or candied yams; braised celery; glazed onions; sauerkraut; cranberry sauce.

Polly Hamblet's Roast Half Turkey

Have a turkey split lengthwise. Freeze one half for another occasion, if you like. Fill the other half turkey with the stuffing of your choice (see pages 169–175) and lay, stuffed side down, on a well-buttered piece of cooking parchment or foil. Sear in a preheated oven at 475°F (245°C), then turn the heat down to 350°F (175°C) and roast, allowing 15 minutes a pound. Baste every 15 minutes. The parchment or foil will enable you to lift the bird from the pan with the stuffing intact.

A half turkey of 8 pounds (3½ kg) will serve six at dinner, with leftovers for the next day.

Roast Turkey Breast

The average turkey breast available at the market comes from smaller turkeys and weighs about 2½ pounds (1125 g), enough to serve up to four people. To serve more than that, try to locate a breast weighing about 4 to 5 pounds (1¾ to 2¼ kg). Rub it well with butter, salt, freshly ground black pepper, and a little thyme or rosemary. Place on a rack, skin side down, and roast 13 to 15 minutes per pound in a 325°F (165°C) oven. Baste frequently, turning once or twice.

VARIATIONS
Spit and balance the breast, and roast over medium coals, basting often with melted butter and a little thyme, allowing 15 minutes per pound (25 minutes per kg), or until nicely browned and just tender.

Turkey Wings Teriyaki

4 whole turkey wings, about 4¾ pounds (2¼ kg)
Cooking oil
2 to 3 cups (½–¾ L) soy sauce
¼ cup (½ dL) sweet sherry
2 tablespoons minced ginger root
2 large garlic cloves, minced
1 tablespoon grated orange rind

Preheat the oven to 375°F (190°C).

Cut each wing into three portions at the joints, reserving the wing tips for use in stock at another time. Dip the remaining portions in oil and place in a single layer in a small roasting pan. Roast, uncovered, in the preheated oven for 45 minutes. Stir together the remaining ingredients and pour over the wings.

Cover tightly with foil and continue baking at the same temperature until tender, about 45 minutes. Serve with rice.

Serves four.

Turkey Broth

Carcass from a roast
   turkey, plus neck and
   giblets (optional) and
   any leftover skin
1 onion, stuck with 3 cloves
2 to 3 carrots, unpeeled

Celery leaves
1 clove garlic
$1/2$ teaspoon dried thyme
6 peppercorns
Cold water to cover
Salt

Place all the ingredients except the salt in a large kettle. Bring
to a boil and simmer for 2 hours, or until you have a rich, well-
flavored broth; season to taste. Skim the fat off the broth and
strain through two thicknesses of cheesecloth.

VARIATION
Bring the broth to a boil. Add noodles, and cook gently until
tender. Serve with slices of hard-boiled egg and plenty of
toasted French bread.

Poached Turkey

Prepare a turkey as for roasting (see page 82). When the bird
is stuffed and trussed, wrap it securely in a heavily floured cloth
and tie it well. Place in a large kettle and cover with boiling,
salted water. Simmer for 3 to $3\frac{1}{2}$ hours, according to the size
of the bird. Unwrap, remove strings and skewers, and serve surrounded by grilled sausages.

A béchamel sauce (page 179) may be served with this. Add
the chopped cooked giblets and 3 tablespoons chopped parsley
to the sauce. Or serve with a hollandaise sauce (page 180) and
steamed rice.

Poached Turkey in Parchment

Butter a turkey and secure 2 or 3 thin slices smoked ham to the
breast. Place in a parchment cooking bag and tie securely. Place
in a deep kettle and cover with boiling water. Simmer for 2

to 3 hours, according to the size of the bird. Serve hot with a giblet sauce or cold with a rémoulade sauce (page 156), cold sliced tongue, and cole slaw. With a decorative garnish, a cold poached turkey makes a handsome and unusual dish for a buffet.

Broiled Turkey

Turkeys weighing from 3 to 6 pounds (1⅓–2¾ kg) are best for broiling. Split them lengthwise, rub well with butter, and place, skin side down, on a broiling rack. Set about 3 inches (7½ cm) from the heat in a broiler preheated to 350°F (175°C). Broil until nicely browned, basting frequently with melted butter. Turn, season with salt and freshly ground black pepper to taste, and brown well again, continuing to baste. This will take from 30 to 45 minutes.

One broiler will serve four to six, depending upon the size of the bird.

VARIATIONS
1. Add finely chopped, cooked giblets to the basting butter for the last 10 minutes of cooking.
2. Sprinkle heavily with chopped parsley when removed from broiler.
3. Baste with olive oil and chopped garlic.

Braised Turkey

1 small turkey, about 8 to 10 pounds (3½– 4½ kg)
8 tablespoons (115 g) butter
Salt and freshly ground black pepper

2 cups (½ L) broth, made from the neck and giblets
1 cup (¼ L) dry white wine
2 tablespoons chopped parsley

Preheat the oven to 350°F (175°C).
Wipe the turkey with a damp cloth, and truss (page 82). Brown it quickly on all sides in the butter in a deep ovenproof casserole or roasting pan. Season with salt and pepper to taste. Add the broth (reserve the giblets) and the wine. Cover the casserole or roasting pan with cooking parchment or foil and tie

securely; or cover with a lid and seal with a thick paste made with flour and water. Place in the preheated oven and cook till the turkey is tender, allowing 20 to 25 minutes per pound (36 to 45 minutes per kg).

Remove the turkey to a hot platter, detaching all strings and skewers. Let the broth cook down very briskly. Degrease, and add the reserved cooked giblets, chopped, the parsley, and salt and pepper to taste. Serve with buttered noodles.

Serves six to eight.

Braised Turkey Wings

4 pounds (1¾ kg) turkey
    wings, with tips
    removed
8 tablespoons (115 g)
    butter

1 cup (¼ L) chicken or
    turkey broth
Salt and freshly ground
    black pepper to taste

Brown the turkey wings in butter in a heavy pot or flameproof casserole. Season to taste and add the broth. Cover tightly and cook over low heat for about 45 minutes, or until tender when tested with a fork. The wings can also be cooked in a 350°F (175°C) oven.

Serves four.

VARIATIONS

With white wine and tarragon: Brown the wings in butter, then pour in ½ cup (1 dL) dry white wine and ½ cup (1dL) chicken or turkey broth. Add 2 tablespoons fresh tarragon or 2 teaspoons dried, and salt lightly to taste. Cover and cook as directed above. Just before serving, add a few drops of freshly squeezed lemon juice.

Provençal: Brown the wings in 6 tablespoons olive oil. Add 1 can (1 pound; 454 g) tomatoes, peeled, seeded, and chopped; 2 cloves garlic, finely chopped; 1 tablespoon chopped fresh basil or a pinch of dried thyme. Salt lightly to taste. Cover and cook as directed above.

Chili: Brown the turkey wings in 3 tablespoons (45 g) butter and 3 tablespoons oil. Add 1 large onion, finely chopped; 2 or

3 cloves garlic, finely chopped; 1½ tablespoons chili powder; 1 hot pepper, cut in strips; ½ cup (1 dL) tomato paste; ½ cup (1 dL) chicken or turkey broth; ½ teaspoon dried basil; and a pinch of powdered coriander. Season with salt to taste. Cover and cook as directed above. Before serving, correct the seasoning and add a few ripe olives. If you like, thicken the sauce with beurre manié (bits of flour and butter kneaded together).

Mabelle's Turkey Casserole

1 small turkey, about 7
    pounds (3¼ kg), cut
    up
Flour
Salt and freshly ground
    black pepper
8 tablespoons (115 g)
    butter

½ pound (225 g) bacon,
    diced
½ cup (60 g) chopped
    shallots or green onion
2 cups (½ L) turkey broth,
    made from the neck
    and giblets

Preheat the oven to 325°F (165°C).

Dredge turkey pieces with flour, salt, and pepper. Melt the butter in a large skillet and brown a few turkey pieces at a time. Transfer to a large ovenproof casserole. Add the bacon, chopped shallots or green onion, and broth. Cover the casserole and allow to simmer in the preheated oven for 1½ to 2 hours, or until the turkey is tender. Taste for seasoning. If you want, thicken the sauce with beurre manié (bits of flour and butter kneaded together). Serve with hot cornbread and succotash.

Serves six to eight.

VARIATIONS

1. Omit the bacon and shallots. Add ¼ teaspoon each freshly grated nutmeg and ground ginger. Use 3 cups (¾ L) red wine instead of broth. Just before serving, add 1 cup (170 g) drained canned black cherries and 1 tablespoon grated lemon zest.

2. Twenty minutes before the turkey is done, add ½ cup 20 g) fresh tarragon leaves or 1 tablespoon dried leaves soaked in white wine and drained.

3. Add 1 cup (60 g) mushrooms sautéed in butter.
4. 25 minutes before the dish is done, remove the cover of the casserole and top the turkey with rounds of biscuit dough. Increase the heat to 425°F (220°C).

Turkey and Wild Rice Casserole

1 cup (170 g) wild rice
1 pound (450 g) mush-
    rooms, sliced
1 onion, chopped
6 tablespoons (85 g) butter
3 cups (340 g) diced,
    cooked turkey
½ cup (60 g) sliced
    almonds, blanched
2 teaspoons salt

¼ teaspoon freshly ground
    black pepper
3 cups (¾ L) turkey or
    chicken broth
1½ cups (3½ dL) heavy
    cream
3 tablespoons (15 g)
    freshly grated
    Parmesan cheese

Wash the rice thoroughly and cover with boiling water. Let soak for 1 hour. Drain well.
Preheat the oven to 350°F (175°C).
Sauté the mushrooms and onion in 3 tablespoons (45 g) butter for 10 minutes. Place in a buttered ovenproof casserole, along with the rice, turkey, almonds, and salt and pepper. Add the broth and cream; mix lightly. Cover and bake in the pre-heated oven for 1½ hours. Remove the cover, sprinkle with the cheese, and dot with the remaining butter. Increase the heat to 450°F (230°C) and bake for 5 minutes longer.
Serves six to eight.

Scalloped Turkey with Noodles

8 ounces (225 g) noodles
Slices of cooked turkey and
    stuffing
Hard-boiled eggs
2 cups (½ L) thin béchamel
    sauce (page 179) or
    turkey gravy

Salt and freshly ground
    black pepper
Buttered bread crumbs

Cook noodles in boiling, salted water till tender. Drain. In a buttered casserole, arrange alternating layers of noodles, turkey, and stuffing. Finish with a layer of sliced hard-boiled eggs. Pour béchamel sauce or turkey gravy over this and season to taste. Sprinkle with buttered crumbs and bake in a 400°F (205°C) oven for 20 minutes.

Serves four.

Casserole of Turkey with Rice

9 tablespoons (130 g) unsalted butter

2 medium onions, chopped

½ pound (225 g) firm white mushrooms, sliced

2 cups (225 g) diced, cooked turkey

½ cup (60 g) diced baked ham

1 cup (200 g) crumbled leftover bread stuffing

2 tablespoons chopped parsley

¼ teaspoon dried thyme

Salt and freshly ground black pepper

1 tablespoon curry powder

1 cup (170 g) uncooked rice

2 cups (½ L) hot chicken or turkey broth, or as needed

Melt 8 tablespoons (115 g) butter in a skillet, add the onion, and sauté over medium heat until limp and golden. Add the mushrooms and sauté for 2 or 3 minutes, until just cooked through. Combine in an ovenproof casserole with the turkey, ham, stuffing, parsley, and thyme. Mix well and taste for seasoning. Add salt and pepper if necessary.

Preheat the oven to 375°F (190°C).

Melt the remaining tablespoon (15 g) butter in the skillet, add the curry powder and rice, and sauté lightly over medium heat until the rice is just translucent (curry powder should always be cooked to take away the raw taste before being added to a dish). Add to the casserole, pour in the hot broth, cover the casserole, and bake until the rice is tender and the liquid absorbed—about 25 to 30 minutes. If the rice does not seem quite tender, add a little more heated broth and continue cooking.

Serves four to six.

Turkey Divan

Cover the bottom of a large, flat casserole with cooked (not over-cooked) broccoli. Arrange slices of cooked turkey on top and mask with sauce Mornay (page 180). Sprinkle with grated Parmesan cheese and put under the broiler for a few minutes to glaze.

Curried Leftover Turkey

1 large onion, chopped
2 tablespoons (30 g) butter
1 apple, cored but not
    peeled, finely chopped
1 green pepper, seeded and
    finely chopped
2 tablespoons curry powder
2 cups (½ L) turkey or
    chicken broth

Cooked turkey wings,
    disjointed
Meat from cooked turkey
    legs and thighs, cut
    into pieces
Leftover turkey gravy
Salt and freshly ground
    black pepper
½ cup (60 g) seedless
    white grapes

Sauté the onion in the butter till soft. Add the apple and green pepper and cook till tender. Mix in the curry powder and cook for a few minutes to remove the raw taste. Pour in the broth and simmer for 10 minutes.

Add the turkey pieces and cook until they are heated through. Mix in any leftover turkey gravy. Season to taste and mix in the grapes. Serve with steamed rice, chutney, chopped salted peanuts, thinly sliced cucumbers dressed with oil and vinegar, and baked bananas. Beer is good with this.

Grilled Leftover Turkey Legs

Remove the legs from a roasted turkey. With a sharp knife, cut away the meat from the bone in one piece. Fill with leftover stuffing and tie securely. Dip in beaten egg, then in bread crumbs. Sauté in butter till nicely browned on all sides. Serve with tomato sauce.

Turkey Loaf

2 cups (225 g) pieces of
    cooked turkey
1 cup (200 g) stuffing
Salt and freshly ground
    black pepper
2 egg yolks

½ cup (1 dL) milk
1 cup béchamel sauce (page
    179) or tomato sauce
1 tablespoon grated onion
2 tablespoons chopped
    parsley

Preheat the oven to 350°F (175°C).

Mince the turkey meat in a food processor or put through a grinder. Mix with the stuffing and salt and pepper to taste. Beat the egg yolks well and add the milk. Mix with the turkey, and taste for seasoning. Place in a buttered loaf pan and bake in the preheated oven for 40 minutes.

Prepare a béchamel sauce or a tomato sauce, and season with the onion and parsley. Serve with the unmolded turkey loaf.

Serves four to six.

Turkey Hash

5 tablespoons (70 g) butter
½ cup (60 g) finely
    chopped onion
2 cloves garlic, finely
    chopped
½ green pepper, seeded
    and finely chopped
3 cups (340 g) diced,
    cooked turkey
1 cup (200 g) cooked
    stuffing

Salt and freshly ground
    black pepper
2/3 cup (140 g) pitted
    black olives
½ cup (60 g) toasted
    almonds
2/3 cup (1½ dL) heavy
    cream
Chopped parsley

Melt the butter in a heavy skillet over medium heat, and sauté the onion, garlic, and green pepper until limp and just delicately brown. Add the turkey and stuffing and toss well with the onion and green pepper. Add salt and pepper to taste. Allow the mixture to cook till thoroughly warmed through. Turn, and blend in the olives and almonds. Dribble the cream over all, and let the hash cook down till nicely crusty at the bottom and piping hot. Add the chopped parsley and invert onto a hot platter, or serve from the skillet in which it was made.

Serves six.

Turkey Tonnato

1 ¼ cups (3 dL) homemade mayonnaise (page 181)
1 teaspoon very finely chopped onion
1 can (7 ounces; 198 g) albacore or white-meat tuna, drained

2 anchovies, finely chopped
Cooked turkey breast, thinly sliced
Cherry tomatoes and black olives for garnish

Prepare the mayonnaise and add the onion. Mix with the flaked tuna and anchovies. Marinate for several hours in the refrigerator to mellow the flavors. Arrange the turkey slices on a serving platter, mask with the tuna sauce, and garnish with cherry tomatoes and black olives.

Turkey and Ham in Aspic

2 cups (225 g) shredded, cooked turkey
1 large slice baked ham or 2 large slices cooked tongue, shredded
1 tablespoon (1 envelope) unflavored gelatin
¼ cup (½ dL) cold water

2 cups (½ L) boiling turkey or chicken broth
1 tablespoon lemon juice
2 teaspoons Worcestershire sauce
Salt and freshly ground black pepper
Stuffed olives, sliced
Hard-boiled eggs, sliced

Combine the shredded meats and set aside. Prepare an aspic by dissolving the gelatin in the cold water, then adding the boiling chicken or turkey broth. Stir in the lemon juice, Worcestershire sauce, and salt and pepper to taste. Allow to cool.

Pour a thin layer of the aspic in a 6-cup ring mold and cool it until it is firm. Place a ring of sliced, stuffed olives and sliced hard-boiled eggs on the gelatin. Then add the shreds of turkey and ham or tongue. Pour the remaining aspic mixture over all and allow it to chill. Unmold on a large plate. Fill the center with either cole slaw or beet and egg salad, dressed with vinai-grette dressing.

Serves four.

Creamed Turkey and Turkey Salads

For creamed turkey dishes and turkey salads, follow the recipes given for chicken.

Cold Turkey for Buffets

Turkey is an ideal buffet food, although it has been overworked in that role. Serve thinly sliced on a platter, garnished with fresh vegetables, olives, or pickles, or serve in combination with either sliced ham or sliced tongue, along with mustard, hot or sweet. Or prepare a wide assortment of turkey sandwiches, following the recipes for chicken given on pages 66–68. Turkey tonnato (page 93) makes a nice change from the usual presentation.

Smoked Turkey

FOR HORS D'OEUVRES

Serve smoked turkey either hot or cold, carved from the bird as needed; or serve in any of the following ways:

Place thin slices of turkey on fingers of buttered pumpernickel or rye.

Combine strips of smoked turkey and Swiss cheese.

Spear cubes of turkey and avocado on small wooden skewers and dip in Russian dressing.

Mix cubes of turkey with chopped walnuts, celery, and mayonnaise, and serve on hot toast.

OTHER USES

Serve sliced cold as a buffet dish along with a complementary meat like tongue or pork (never ham or beef).

Cut into julienne for a chef's salad or an avocado and grapefruit salad.

Dice and make into smoked turkey hash (see Turkey Hash, page 92).

NORTH AMERICAN WILD TURKEY

The North American wild turkey is, as its name implies, truly American. It should be prepared with simplicity. To begin with, this bird differs from its domestic kin in shape, size, and flavor. It has an enormously deep breast and longer legs, and the dark meat is as epicurean as the light. Seldom exceeding 12 to 15 pounds (5½–6¾ kg) for the toms, and 10 to 12 pounds (4½–5½ kg) for the hens, it is built for speed both in running and gliding to cover. Rare now in its native habitats—the source of supply is for the most part through game farms—it is as difficult and sporting a game bird to hunt as woodcock.

As for flavor, it differs as much from the domestic turkey as, for example, the mallard does from the Pekin duck. It can not be said to have a gamy taste, as does the pheasant or quail. But the rich difference is there, and is greatly preferred to the flavor of domestic varieties. Contrary to most other game birds, the flesh is juicy, not dry.

The preparation is in principle similar to the roasting of any domestic bird. It should be stuffed with only the simplest ingredients: dry bread crumbs added to finely chopped onions, leeks, and celery, which have been lightly sautéed in butter. Mix all together until well blended, adding salt and pepper, and last the liver (gizzard, too, if you like it) which has been poached and chopped. Simmer the gizzard and the neck together with a little water to make a broth, and set aside for addition to the gravy after the bird is done.

Stuff the bird with this mixture, and do not worry if the dressing seems dry; it picks up plenty of moisture from the turkey while cooking, and a soggy dressing is insufferable. Roast until done in a 350°F (175°C) oven, basting at least every 15 minutes. It needs no cover, or larding, but it must be basted constantly for a perfect glaze. Never add water to a roasting bird. When done remove the turkey to a hot platter and keep warm while making the gravy. Use the roasting pan and pour off excess fat, of which there should be plenty. Add the broth from the neck and gizzard, and be sure to dissolve the little brown pieces stuck to the pan; that is where the best flavor is. Add salt and freshly ground black pepper to taste. And just before serving, swirl a little butter in it, which thickens it just enough. Wild turkey needs no dressing up; it is quite good enough of itself to bring out its own flavor. Serve with boiled and well-buttered hominy or samp, and braised leeks, or the tenderest kale.

A fine California Cabernet or a good French Burgundy will complement this truly wonderful bird.

3

Duck

The duck commonly available in this country is the Long Island strain, developed with a heavy layer of fat, which produces a juicier, tenderer bird but gives relatively little meat for its size. Thus a duck of 4 to 5 pounds (1¾–2¼ kg) will feed only two people well. For the best results, the Long Island should be roasted in a moderate oven for sufficient time to allow the fat to render. The skin can be crisped by roasting at high heat for the final period of cooking.

Most Long Island ducks are sold frozen and should be thawed before cooking. This will take 1 to 1½ days in the refrigerator, 4 to 5 hours at room temperature, or 2 to 3 hours in cool water.

Fresh-killed ducks can often be found in Chinese markets, with head and feet intact, and sometimes in country markets. In Pennsylvania one finds Muscovy duck, which is a leaner but tougher bird than the Long Island and is best when braised. Generally, most of the population will encounter nothing during their lifetime except frozen Long Island duckling.

Roast Duckling

1 duckling, 4 to 5 pounds (1¾–2¼ kg)
Salt and freshly ground black pepper

Dried thyme or rosemary
1 onion, stuck with 2 cloves

Preheat the oven to 350°F (175°C).

Rub the duckling with salt and pepper and thyme or rosemary. Place the onion in the cavity. Set the duckling on a rack in a roasting pan. Roast in the preheated oven, allowing 1 hour for rare duck, 1½ hours for medium rare, and 2 hours for well done. After 30 minutes of roasting, prick the skin all over several times to release the fat. If you like a crisp skin, increase the heat to 500°F (260°C) for the final 15 minutes of roasting and cut the total roasting time by 5 minutes.

To test for doneness, prick the thigh joint with a fork. If the juices run pink, the duck should be medium rare; if they run clear, it should be well done.

Duck does not lend itself to carving, and it is best to cut it into halves or quarters with poultry shears.

One duckling will feed two people.

VARIATIONS:

With curry and honey: Mix ¼ cup (½ dL) honey with 1½ tablespoons curry powder. After the duck has cooked for 1 hour, brush at intervals with this mixture to give the skin a nice glaze.

Au poivre: Half an hour before the duck is done, remove it from the oven and press 1 tablespoon coarsely ground black pepper into the skin. Return to the oven to finish roasting.

Roast Duck with Oranges

1 duck, 4 to 5 pounds
   (1¾–2¼ kg)
1 clove garlic
2 oranges, peeled and
   separated into sections
Salt and freshly ground
   black pepper

1 cup (¼ L) orange juice
1 tablespoon grated orange
   zest
¼ cup (½ dL) orange
   liqueur
1½ teaspoons (7 g) butter

Preheat the oven to 350°F (175°C).

Insert the garlic and orange sections in the cavity of the duck. Rub the skin with salt and pepper. Place on a rack in a roasting pan and roast as directed in the preceding recipe, basting several times with orange juice. When the bird is done, transfer to a warm platter while you prepare the sauce.

Skim the excess fat from the roasting pan and add the orange zest, remaining orange juice, and orange liqueur. Reduce the sauce over high heat until it has thickened slightly. Add salt and pepper to taste and swirl in the butter. Cut the duck into quarters and serve with the oranges and sauce.

Serves two to three.

Roast Duck with Sauerkraut

½ cup (60 g) finely diced salt pork
1 medium onion, finely chopped
1 apple, finely chopped
Salt and freshly ground black pepper to taste
1 sprig thyme
Caraway seeds
2 pounds (900 g) sauerkraut
2 ducks, 5 pounds (2¼ kg) each
White wine

Preheat the oven to 350°F (175°C).

Try out the salt pork in a skillet. Add the onion and apple and sauté gently, then add salt and pepper. Add the thyme and a few caraway seeds; then add the sauerkraut. Mix well and stuff the ducks with the mixture. Sew up the vents.

Place the ducks, breast side up, on a trivet in a roasting pan. Place in the preheated oven and roast according to the directions on page 99, basting with wine several times. Remove the ducks to a hot platter. Skim the excess fat from the pan and let the sauce cook down for 3 minutes. Pour around the ducks and serve with a potato purée.

Serves four.

Duck with Olives

2 ducks, 5 pounds (2¼ kg) each, necks and giblets reserved
1 onion, stuck with 2 cloves
2 carrots
1 bay leaf
Salt and freshly ground black pepper
Sprigs of parsley
10 to 12 cloves garlic
1½ cups (340 g) small unpitted green olives
Beurre manié (a little flour and butter kneaded together)

Prepare 2 cups (½ L) broth by simmering for 1 hour, in water to cover, the neck and giblets of the duck, the onion stuck with the cloves, the carrots, bay leaf, and salt and pepper to taste.

Preheat the oven to 350°F (175°C).

Rub the ducks with a damp cloth. Place several sprigs of parsley and 5 or 6 garlic cloves in the cavity of each duck, then place on a trivet in a shallow pan. Roast in the preheated oven, allowing 18 to 20 minutes per pound. After 30 minutes, prick the skin all over; baste once or twice with broth. Thirty minutes before the duck is done, increase the temperature to 450°F (230°C) to crisp the skin. Twenty minutes later, add the green olives. When the duck is tender, season with salt and pepper to taste and remove to a hot platter. Skim the excess fat from the pan and add the remaining broth. Reduce over high heat, and thicken with beurre manié added in small bits, and salt and pepper to taste. Pour the sauce with the olives around the duck.

Serves four.

Casserole of Duck with Yogurt

2 ducks, 5 pounds (2¼ kg) each, giblets reserved and chopped
Flour for dredging
¼ cup (½ dL) oil or 4 tablespoons (60 g) butter
Salt and freshly ground black pepper to taste
2 medium onions, finely chopped
3 tablespoons chopped parsley
Pinch of dried rosemary
Pinch of dried thyme
1 clove garlic, peeled
2 cups (½ L) white wine
1 cup yogurt

Preheat the oven to 350°F (175°C).

Cut up the duck in convenient serving pieces (carving shears are a great help here). Prick the skin well. Dredge the pieces with flour and sear them well in oil or butter. Drain on paper towels and transfer to an ovenproof casserole. Season with salt and pepper to taste. Add the chopped giblets, onion, parsley, rosemary, thyme, and garlic. Pour in the white wine and cover the casserole. Place in the preheated oven and cook for 1½ hours. Test for tenderness. If necessary, continue cooking until done, about 30 minutes more. Remove the duck to a hot platter. Skim off excess fat from the pan juices, add the yogurt, and heat through; do not allow to boil. Correct the seasoning. Serve with rice and buttered turnips.

Serves four to six.

Casserole of Duck with Red Cabbage

2 ducks, 5 pounds (2¼ kg) each
Flour for dredging
Salt and freshly ground black pepper
6 tablespoons cooking oil or butter
1 onion, finely chopped
Caraway seeds
Pinch of dried sweet basil
1 medium head red cabbage, shredded
3 tablespoons wine vinegar
2 tablespoons brown sugar

Preheat the oven to 350°F (175°C).

Skin and cut up the ducks into convenient serving pieces. Dredge with flour, salt, and pepper. Brown in ¼ cup (½ dL) oil or 4 tablespoons (60 g) butter, drain on paper towels, and transfer the pieces to an ovenproof casserole. Add the onion, a few caraway seeds, sweet basil, and bake in the preheated oven for 30 minutes.

While the duck is cooking, heat the remaining oil or butter in the skillet in which you browned the duck and add the red cabbage. Cook down quickly for 10 minutes, tossing it well. Add the wine vinegar, brown sugar, and salt and pepper to taste. Simmer for 5 minutes. Add to the casserole, cover, and simmer till the ducks are tender, about 1 hour more. Serve with potato pancakes.

Serves four to six.

Casserole of Duck with Pinto Beans

2 cups (450 g) dried brown
    pinto beans
2 cloves garlic
1 bay leaf
1 onion, stuck with 2 cloves
2 ducks, 5 pounds (2¼ kg)
    each
Flour for dredging

Salt and freshly ground
    black pepper
2 tablespoons (30 g) butter
3 slices salt pork, diced
2 medium onions, finely
    chopped
Pinch of dried sweet basil
½ teaspoon dry mustard

Soak the pinto beans overnight (or follow directions on the package). Drain, then add the garlic, bay leaf, and onion. Cover with boiling, salted water and cook until tender. Drain, reserving the liquid.

Preheat the oven to 350°F (175°C).

Skin and cut up the ducks in convenient serving pieces. Cut the skin in thin strips and set aside. Dredge the duck in flour seasoned with salt and pepper. Melt the butter in a skillet and try out the salt pork. Add the chopped onion and sauté till limp. Transfer the pieces of salt pork and the onion to a casserole. Sear the duck in the salt pork fat and also transfer to the casserole.

Add the beans, sweet basil, freshly ground black pepper, and dry mustard. Mix the duck with the beans. Pour in enough bean liquid to cover and let simmer, covered, in the preheated oven, till the beans and duck are thoroughly tender, about 2 hours. Add more liquid if it cooks away too quickly.

Deep-fry the strips of skin in oil heated to 355°F (180°C) for 2 to 3 minutes to crisp. Drain. Use as garnish for the duck.

Serves six.

Braised Duck with Port

1 duck, 5 pounds (2¼ kg)
Stuffing of your choice (see
    pages 169–175)
¼ cup (½ dL) cooking oil
    or 4 tablespoons
    (60 g) butter
2 slices lemon

1 cup (¼ L) port, more
    as needed
2 tablespoons grated orange
    zest
1 teaspoon lemon juice
Salt and freshly ground
    black pepper to taste

Preheat the oven to 350°F (175°C).

Stuff the duck, and sew up or skewer the vent. Brown in the oil or butter. Transfer to an ovenproof casserole and add lemon slices and port. Cover and braise in the preheated oven for 2 hours, basting with additional wine three or four times during the cooking. Prick the skin with a fork to release the fat. When the duck has achieved the proper degree of tenderness, remove it to a hot platter and skim all excess fat from the casserole. Add the orange zest and lemon juice and reduce the sauce. Correct the seasoning and pour around the duck. Serve with wild rice.

Serves two.

Broiled Duckling

Split a 4- to 5-pound (1¾–2¼ kg) duckling down the back or have the butcher do it for you. Wash and thoroughly dry, then place, skin side down, in a preheated 350°F (175°C) broiler 6 inches (15 cm) from the heat. Broil for 18 minutes. Turn, prick the skin, and continue broiling for 15 to 18 minutes, watching carefully. Salt and pepper well on each side. Serve with wild rice, green salad, and a good Beaujolais.

Serves two.

Duckling au Poivre

1 duckling, 4 to 5 pounds (1¾–2¼ kg), split in half, wings removed	1 teaspoon salt 1 tablespoon crushed black peppercorns
½ lemon	

Rub the bone side of the duck with half a lemon, and sprinkle the skin side with salt. Arrange, bone side up, on a rack in a broiling pan. Broil 6 inches from the heating unit for 20 minutes. Turn, prick the surface of the skin well with a fork, and continue broiling for 10 minutes. Remove and press the skin side of each half into the crushed peppercorns, using wadded paper towels to protect your hands. Broil, skin side up, for another 10 to 15 minutes, or until browned and crisp.

Serves two.

Duck Mayonnaise

2 ducklings, 5 pounds (2¼ kg) each
2 onions, each stuck with 1 or 2 cloves
4 carrots
1 bay leaf
3 to 4 stalks celery
Bouquet garni (1 sprig thyme, 1 sprig parsley, few leaves tarragon and rosemary, and a few juniper berries, tied in cheesecloth)
Salt and freshly ground black pepper
Cold water to cover
Romaine leaves
Homemade mayonnaise (page 181)
Garnishes (see below)

Place the ducks in a deep kettle with the onions, carrots, bay leaf, celery, bouquet garni, and salt and pepper to taste. Cover with cold water, bring to a boil, then reduce the heat and simmer till the ducks are tender, about 1½ hours. Remove from the broth and cool. Save the broth for soups or for aspic jelly (see below).

Skin the ducks and cut into convenient serving pieces, removing the bones. Arrange on a chilled platter nicely covered with leaves of romaine. Spoon the mayonnaise over the duck. Garnish with capers, chopped parsley, tomato quarters, hard-boiled eggs, and pimiento strips. Serve with more mayonnaise.

Serves six.

VARIATION:

Duck in Aspic: Strain 4 cups (1 L) of the degreased broth through cheesecloth, return it to a small saucepan, and add the beaten white of an egg and the shell. Bring to a boil; strain again.

Melt 2 tablespoons (2 envelopes) unflavored gelatin in ½ cup (1 dL) cold water. Add to the boiling broth and stir till the gelatin is thoroughly blended. Add 1 tablespoon lemon juice and a few grains of cayenne. Cool until almost jellied. Dip each piece of duck in the jelly and set aside to chill. Arrange on a platter and garnish with mayonnaise and tomatoes and cucumber. Chop the remaining jelly in small cubes and arrange around the platter. If you like, cut the skin into strips, deep-fry (see page 104), and use as a garnish. Serve with a green salad.

WILD DUCK

No two people seem to agree upon the proper length of time to cook a wild duck. There is the cook-till-the-flesh-falls-off-the bones school; and those happy in-betweens who just like to eat wild duck because it sounds nice. I like mine rare with some blood running.

Over a hundred varieties of wild duck are known, but the choice we are usually given is rather limited. The most common are the mallard, the canvasback, the teal—all excellent in their ways. The teal is quite small—in fact some of my friends have been known to eat two and even three at a meal.

Wild ducks are sometimes hell to pick. They are more often than not covered with pin feathers that stick like glue. Singe the birds well, sit down with a pair of tweezers and do the best you can. Draw the wild duck as you would any other bird, taking special caution not to break the gall bladder.

If you are of the long-cooking school, you will want a savory stuffing for your birds. Choose any stuffing you like, although I have given a simple stuffing (page 173) that goes admirably with duck.

One-half duck usually constitutes a serving unless the birds are very small, when a whole one, or possibly two, is the required portion. Carving shears are a must with all kinds of game birds.

Wild ducks can be roasted or braised in the manner of domestic ducks, if you so desire (see pages 99 to 104), but they will not be as satisfactory.

Wild rice or fried hominy, turnips, and green peas are traditional accompaniments. Some people insist on a tart jelly. I hate it. I'd much rather have a mellow, well-rounded wine to enhance the flavor of the duck, such as a California Cabernet or a fine French Burgundy.

Leftover wild duck may be made into a salmi or used as you would domestic duck. It is delicious cold with a salad.

Roast Wild Duck I

Singe, pick, and clean the ducks. Insert a sprig of parsley or a few juniper berries in the vent of each, if you like. Place on a rack in a shallow roasting pan and rub the breasts with butter. For blood-rare, roast in a preheated 475° to 500°F (245°–260°C) oven 15 to 20 minutes, depending upon the size of the ducks. Baste every 5 minutes with melted butter or a mixture of melted butter and red wine. Season with salt and pepper to taste and remove to a hot platter. These birds will give plenty of rich, red juices when a sharp knife is sunk into the breasts.

Roast Wild Duck II

Singe and clean each duck, and stuff it if you wish. (Do not use a stuffing containing pork unless previously cooked.) Close the vent and tie a piece of larding pork around the breast. Place on a rack in a roasting pan, breast side up, and roast in a preheated 350°F (175°C) oven, allowing 15 minutes to the pound (27 minutes per kg). Baste with melted butter or red wine. Many people prefer to cover the ducks when roasting this way, but I do not advise it.

Oregon Wild Duck

Stuff a duck with pieces of onion, celery, and apple. Close the vent with a piece of foil. Salt and pepper the breast and lay a piece of bacon across it. Roast on a rack in a roasting pan in a hot (400°F or 205°C) oven, 45 minutes for a large duck and less time for teal or small ducks. Baste occasionally with red wine. This results in a juicy but not bloody bird.

Traditionally this duck was served with elderberry jelly and wild rice. The rice is excellent with a duck gravy made thus:

1 onion, finely chopped
Gizzard and heart of the duck, chopped
3 tablespoons (45 g) butter
2 cups (½ L) boiling water
Pan drippings
Beurre manié (a little flour and butter kneaded together)
Freshly ground black pepper
Pinch of cayenne
¼ cup (½ dL) Cognac

Sauté the onion with the chopped heart and gizzard in the butter. Add the boiling water and simmer for perhaps an hour. Add the pan drippings from the roast and thicken with the beurre manié, added in bits. Season highly with pepper, and add cayenne and Cognac.

Broiled Wild Duck

Small young ducks may be broiled either split or whole. Rub well with butter or oil and place on a rack in a preheated broiler, skin side down, if split; on one side, if whole. Broil for 10 to 20 minutes, depending upon how well done you like your duck. Turn frequently, especially if you are broiling a whole bird.

Mary Frost Mabon's St. Louis Wild Ducks

Mary Frost Mabon, who used to write for *Harper's Bazaar* as their food and wine editor and wrote several cookbooks, was a great fancier of good food. Here is her version of an old family recipe:

"These ducks are cooked on the top of the stove in a thin aluminum pan, of a size to hold two ducks. First make as hot a fire as your stove will give. Then melt enough fat (one-half lard, one-half butter) in your pan to half cover your birds. When this boils in the pan over the very hot fire put in the ducks breast-side down, cover with a lid (but see to it this is so placed that steam can escape). Leave this for 7 minutes, then remove the lid and turn the birds over. After they are turned pour 2 tablespoons of Italian vermouth over the breasts, then put the lid on and allow to cook for another 7 minutes. Take off the lid again, turn the ducks over on their breasts again, pour a little vermouth over their backs and let them stay there 2 minutes.

"Now turn the birds again and test with a fork. If blood comes out, they must be turned again for 2 minutes. If a clear liquid comes out they are done. Remove the birds to a warm pan while you cool the contents left in the aluminum pan quickly by setting it in a dishpan filled with ice and water. The fat can then be rapidly poured off, or removed from the top. The juice will be left; add to it previously prepared sliced orange peel with salt, pepper, paprika, 2 tablespoons of vermouth and as much currant jelly as you fancy. Heat, pour over your birds on a deep platter and bear triumphantly to the carver."

Note: Quail can be cooked the same way in a smaller pan, with 1 ½ minute turnings.

Wild Duck in the Mud

If you just can't wait till you return to civilization, choose a young duck from your catch, remove the head, slit the vent, and draw the entrails. Wash thoroughly. Salt and pepper the cavity and in it place an apple or an onion. Roll the whole thing, feathers and all, in thick, gooey (but clean-smelling) mud or clay. It should be caked on thickly to make it airtight. Place in hot coals or on a grill over a brisk fire until the mud or clay dries out. Split the coating and remove; the feathers will come along with it. Add a little butter and salt and pepper, and eat away.

4

Squab & Pigeon

Squab and pigeon appear in our markets in more or less limited quantities, but their distinctive flavor makes them well worth considering as a change from the other poultry and game birds. They weigh from ¾ pound to 1¼ pounds (340–565 g) and are served either whole or split and butterflied, usually one to a person. They can be roasted, broiled, or sautéed and more or less call for eating with the fingers.

Roast Squab

Stuff the squab, if you wish (see pages 169–175), and butter well or cover the breast with bacon. Roast on a rack in a pre-heated 400°F (205°C) oven from 30 to 40 minutes, or until tender. Test by pricking the thigh joint to see if the juices run clear. The birds should be rather well done. Season with salt and pepper to taste. Serve on well-browned fried hominy squares.

Broiled Squab

Split the squab down the back and flatten it out. Rub well with butter or other fat, place on a rack, and broil for 15 minutes, turning once. Season with salt and pepper to taste.

Squab may be broiled whole, but they must be turned often to get an even color on all sides. Give them 20 minutes. Serve one to a person. You'll have to use your fingers to nibble bits from the bone.

Broiled Squab with Rosemary Butter

Follow the recipe for broiled chicken with rosemary butter (page 32). Remove the backbone and flatten the squab. Broil bone side up for 8 minutes, then turn and broil for another 6 minutes.

Squab Sauté with Bacon

1 squab, split and flattened
Salt and freshly ground
    black pepper

6 to 8 slices bacon
Chopped parsley

Salt and pepper the squab. Sauté the bacon slices in a skillet till crisp. Remove the bacon and keep hot. Gently sauté the squab in the bacon fat for 15 to 20 minutes, or until the bird is tender. Sprinkle with chopped parsley and serve with the crisp bacon slices.

    Serves 1.

Squab Sauté with White Wine and Herbs

8 tablespoons (115 g)
    butter or other fat
4 small squabs, split down
    the back and flattened
Salt and freshly ground
    black pepper
¼ cup (30 g) chopped
    shallots

1½ cups (3½ dL) white
    wine
¼ cup (15 g) chopped
    parsley
2 tablespoons fresh tarragon
    or 2 teaspoons dried
4 slices crisp buttered toast

Heat 4 tablespoons (60 g) butter or other fat in each of two skillets and brown the squab halves on both sides over a brisk flame. Add salt and pepper to taste. To each skillet add half the chopped shallots and ½ cup (1 dL) white wine. Reduce the heat and cover the pans. Simmer for 15 minutes. Add 2 tablespoons chopped parsley and 1 tablespoon fresh tarragon or 1 teaspoon dried to each pan. Add a little more wine—about ½ cup (1 dL) altogether—and cook, uncovered, for 5 minutes. Serve on crisp buttered toast with the sauce spooned over.

    Serves four.

Squab Sauté with Cabbage and Yogurt

4 small squabs, split down
    the back and flattened
8 tablespoons (115 g)
    butter or other fat
Salt and freshly ground
    black pepper

1 small head cabbage, very
    finely shredded
1 cup (¼ L) yogurt
Chopped parsley

Heat 4 tablespoons of butter in each of two skillets and brown the squab on both sides, then reduce the heat and sauté till tender, about 18 to 20 minutes, turning twice. Add salt and pepper to taste. Four to 8 minutes before the squab is done, cook the cabbage in boiling salted water until tender. Drain, add salt to taste and the yogurt, and mix well. Arrange on a large platter and place the squab halves on it. Sprinkle with chopped parsley and serve.

Serves four.

Casserole of Squab with Tomatoes

1 can (28 ounces; 794 g)
    Italian plum tomatoes
5 small onions
6 tablespoons (85 g) butter
Salt and freshly ground
    black pepper
4 squabs
Parsley
6 slices bacon, diced

1 clove garlic, finely
    chopped
1 medium onion, very finely
    chopped
Pinch of dried thyme
Pinch of dried sweet basil
1 cup (60 g) sliced mush-
    rooms

Prepare a tomato sauce by putting the plum tomatoes through a food mill and reducing over medium heat with 1 small chopped onion until thickened. Stir in the butter, and add salt and pepper to taste. You should have about 2 cups of sauce.

Preheat the oven to 350°F (175°C).

Stuff each squab with a small onion and several sprigs of parsley. Try out the bacon in a skillet. Remove the bacon and brown the squab in the fat very quickly, along with the garlic. Place the birds in a deep ovenproof casserole with the finely chopped onion, thyme, basil, mushrooms, and tomato sauce.

Cover the casserole and simmer in the preheated oven for 1 hour, or until the birds are tender. Taste the sauce for seasoning. Serve with buttered noodles sprinkled with grated Parmesan cheese.

Serves four.

Casserole of Pigeon with Rice

4 young pigeons
¾ cups (1¾ dL) olive oil
Salt and freshly ground
    black pepper
2 onions, finely chopped
2 cloves garlic, finely
    chopped

1 green pepper, seeded and
    cut in thin strips
Chicken broth
1½ cups (255 g) raw rice
½ cup (115 g) pine nuts
½ cup (30 g) sliced mush-
    rooms
3 pimientos, cut in thin strips

Preheat the oven to 350°F (175°C).

Singe, draw, and clean the pigeons. Leave whole, or split, if you prefer. Heat ½ cup (1 dL) olive oil in a flameproof casserole and brown the pigeons well on all sides. Season with salt and pepper to taste, then add the onion, garlic, green pepper, and ½ cup (1 dL) chicken broth. Cover the casserole and simmer in the preheated oven for 20 minutes—1 hour, for older pigeons.

Brown the raw rice very lightly in the remaining ¼ cup (½ dL) oil. Add to the casserole, along with the pine nuts, sliced mushrooms, and pimientos. Cover the whole with hot chicken broth. Replace in the oven, uncovered, and cook until the rice is tender and the broth is entirely cooked away. More broth may be added, if necessary.

Serves four to six.

Casserole of Wood Pigeon with Sauerkraut

Wood pigeon, which used to be bountiful in the markets, is seldom found nowadays. However, people do shoot them in season and find them somewhat less tender than squab. Therefore they require longer, slower cooking.

4 wood pigeons
5 tablespoons (70 grams)
    bacon fat
Salt and freshly ground
    black pepper to taste
1 teaspoon dried thyme
½ teaspoon dried marjoram

1½ cups (3½ dL) dry
    white wine
2 pounds (900 g) sauer-
    kraut
4 tart apples, peeled and
    quartered
1 teaspoon caraway seeds

Preheat the oven to 350°F (175°C).

Singe, draw, and clean the wood pigeons. Melt the bacon fat in a flameproof casserole and brown the pigeons well on all sides over brisk heat. Add salt and pepper and the thyme, marjoram, and ½ cup (1 dL) wine. Cover the casserole and simmer in the preheated oven for 1 hour.

Drain the sauerkraut. Place it in a kettle with the apples, caraway seeds, and remaining white wine. Simmer over a low flame for 1 hour.

Remove the casserole from the oven. Arrange the sauerkraut around the birds. Cover the casserole and replace in the oven for 1 hour more, or until the pigeons are tender. Add more wine if the dish becomes too dry. Serve with mashed potatoes and more of the white wine, well chilled.

Serves four.

Pigeons in Jelly, a Beautiful Dish

Here is an eighteenth-century recipe for pigeon that I consider one of the most amusing I have ever encountered. Don't try it unless you have infinite patience and great feeling for the surrealist school of cookery.

"Pick two very nice pigeons, and make them look as well as possible by singeing, washing and cleaning the heads well. Leave the heads and the feet on, but clip the nails close to the claws. Roast them of a very nice brown; and when done put a little sprig of myrtle into the bill of each. Have ready a savoury jelly, and with it half fill a bowl that is of a proper size to turn down on the dish you mean it to be served in. When the jelly and the birds are cold, see that no gravy hangs to the birds, and then lay them upside down in the jelly. Before the rest of it begin to set, pour it over the birds, so as to be three inches above the feet. This should be done full twenty-four hours before serving.

"This dish has a very handsome appearance in the middle range of a second course; or when served with the jelly roughed large, it makes a side or corner dish, its size being then less. The head should be kept up as if alive, by tying the neck with some thread, and the legs bent as if the pigeon sat upon them."

5

Goose

Goose has never had great popularity in the United States. Although certain national groups have appreciated goose for generations, the average cook never dreams of buying one except for specific occasions. Even on holidays it is overlooked. The Thanksgiving and Christmas bird is invariably turkey, not goose. Yet since ancient times it has been much prized in Europe, especially in England, Germany, and France. It has been neglected here for perhaps two reasons: it is not a very economical bird, for there is a great deal of fat and a complex bone structure; and birds of good quality have not been generally available. However, an extremely fine goose has now been developed by the National Goose Council. Raised for tenderness and flavor, these are sold quick-frozen throughout the country. Weighing from 6 to 14 pounds (2¾–6¼ kg), they come small enough to fit in anyone's oven.

Frozen goose must be thawed before cooking. There are three recommended ways to do this:

1. Leave the goose in its wrapping, place on a tray, and leave in the refrigerator—1 to 1½ days for a 6- to 10-pound (2¾–4½ kg) bird; about 2 days for a 14-pound (6¼ kg) bird.
2. Leave the goose in its wrapping and immerse in cold water, changing the water often. Depending on the size of the goose, thawing will take 4 to 6 hours.
3. Leave the goose in its wrapping, set on a tray, and thaw at room temperature, which will take 6 to 12 hours.

Goose can be prepared much the same as domestic duck and should have a tart, savory stuffing. Sage is used for goose by many people, but I feel that this herb overpowers most poultry and advise against it. Apples and chestnuts and prunes are welcome ingredients in a goose stuffing (see page 174). Also consider the sauerkraut stuffing on page 174. If you use bread crumbs, be certain that the stuffing is dry, for the goose is fat and juicy and lubricates the cavity as it cooks.

Roast Goose

Remove excess fat from the cavity of an 8- to 10-pound (3½–4½ kg) goose. Stuff with any of the stuffings suggested for goose (see pages 171–174), using ¾ to 1 cup per pound (450 g) of bird. Truss, and sew up or skewer the vent. Rub with salt, and place, breast side up, on a rack in a roasting pan. Roast for 1 hour at 400°F (205°C) in a preheated oven, then prick the skin all over to let the fat drain off. Reduce the temperature to 350°F (175°C) and continue roasting until done, about another 1 to 1¾ hours. Remove the fat from the roasting pan as it accumulates, using a bulb baster or spoon, and reserve; it is an excellent fat for cooking. To test for doneness, prick the thigh joint with a fork. The juices should be clear, with perhaps a tinge of pink. Remove to a hot platter and allow to rest for 15 minutes before carving. Serve with Sauce for Roast Goose.

TO ROAST IN A MICROWAVE OVEN

Cover the legs and wings of the goose with small pieces of foil. (This will not affect the oven, due to the bird's large size.) Place the bird, breast side down, on inverted saucers in a 2-quart (2 L) baking dish, thus holding the goose above and out of the juices. Cook, uncovered, for 30 minutes. Drain off juices and fat. Turn the goose breast side up and remove the foil. Continue cooking for an additional 30 minutes, or until a meat thermometer registers 180°F (82°C) when inserted in the thigh. Remove from the oven, cover with foil, and let stand for about 10 to 15 minutes to allow the goose to finish cooking.

Goose Broth

While the goose is roasting, prepare a stock for gravy or sauce.

Giblets and neck of the
   goose
1 or 2 sprigs parsley
1 onion, stuck with 1 clove

1 carrot, scraped
3 or 4 peppercorns
1 teaspoon salt
Cold water to cover

Combine all the ingredients in a saucepan. Bring to a boil and skim, then reduce the heat and simmer, covered, for 1 hour.

Makes about 2 cups (1/2 L).

Goose Gravy

1/4 cup (60 g) rendered
   goose fat
2 tablespoons flour
2 cups (1/2 L) goose broth
   (see above), heated

Goose liver, sautéed in
   goose fat and
   chopped
Salt and freshly ground
   black pepper to taste

Melt the goose fat in a saucepan. Stir in the flour and blend over low heat for 2 or 3 minutes. Add the broth, increase the heat, and stir until smooth and thickened. Add the chopped liver and salt and pepper to taste, and let simmer for several minutes more.

Makes about 2 1/2 cups (6 dL).

Sauce for Roast Goose

3 tablespoons (45 g)
   rendered goose fat
1 medium onion, finely
   chopped
Goose liver, chopped
2 tablespoons chopped
   parsley
1/2 cup (30 g) chopped
   mushrooms

1 cup (1/4 L) goose broth
   (see above)
1 cup (1/4 L) cream,
   blended with 2 egg
   yolks
2 tablespoons brandy
Salt and freshly ground
   black pepper

Melt the goose fat in a saucepan over medium heat. Sauté the onion until limp. Add the liver, parsley, and mushrooms; sauté for 5 minutes. Add the broth and simmer for 3 or 4 minutes.

Finally add the cream mixed with the egg yolks. Stir constantly over low heat till the mixture thickens (do not allow to boil), and add the brandy. Season to taste.

Makes about 3 cups (¾ L).

Golden State Goose

1 goose, 8 to 10 pounds (3½ to 4½ kg)
4 shallots, chopped
3 tablespoons (45 g) rendered goose fat
2 cups (115 g) fresh bread crumbs
2 tablespoons chopped parsley
Pinch of dried thyme
1 tablespoon plus 1 teaspoon grated orange zest
1 cup (115 g) almonds or walnuts, toasted

Goose liver, chopped
½ cup (1 dL) plus 3 tablespoons sherry
2 oranges, unpeeled and stuck with 3 cloves
Orange juice as needed
1 cup (¼ L) goose broth (see page 122)
1 tablespoon (15 g) butter
1 tablespoon flour
Salt and freshly ground black pepper

Preheat the oven to 400°F (205°C).

Stuff the goose with a stuffing made as follows: Sauté the shallots in the fat; add the bread crumbs, parsley, thyme, 1 tablespoon grated orange zest, nut meats, the chopped goose liver, and ½ cup (1 dL) sherry and mix well. Truss the goose (see page 82) and place on a rack in a roasting pan in which you have placed the oranges stuck with the cloves. Roast according to the directions on page 122, basting two or three times with orange juice.

Remove the goose to a hot platter. Discard the oranges. Skim the fat from the pan juices and add the broth. Set over low heat and stir in a beurre manié (bits of the butter and flour kneaded together) till well mixed and thickened. Add salt and pepper to taste, then add the remaining orange zest and sherry. Carve the goose and serve with the sauce.

Serves 8.

Goose Alsatian Style

1 medium onion, sliced
2 tablespoons (30 g)
    rendered goose fat
2 cups (½ L) dry white
    wine
1 cup (¼ L) water
3 pounds (1350 g) fresh
    sauerkraut
2 cloves garlic, minced
10 juniper berries, tied in a
    cheesecloth bag

Salt and freshly ground
    black pepper to taste
1 pound (450 g) slab bacon
    in 1 piece
2 pig's knuckles, cracked
    (optional)
1 goose, 8 to 10 pounds
    (3½–4½ kg)
¼ cup (30 g) each of finely
    diced carrots, leek or
    onion, and celery
6 to 8 frankfurters

In a large pot, lightly sauté the onion in the fat. Add the wine and the water. Wash the sauerkraut very thoroughly in hot water and add to the pot with the garlic, juniper berries in cheesecloth, salt, pepper, and bacon. Cover and cook slowly for 2 hours. Remove the cheesecloth bag.

Meanwhile, if the pig's knuckles are used, cook them in boiling water until tender. Preheat the oven to 400°F (205°C) and roast the goose as directed on page 122. About 20 minutes before the goose is done, add the finely chopped vegetables to pan; complete the roasting. Heat the frankfurters through. When all is ready, put the sauerkraut on a large platter. Arrange knuckles, sliced bacon, sliced goose, and frankfurters on the sauerkraut. Degrease the juices in the roasting pan, add a little broth or water, and heat. Season to taste. Pour, with the diced vegetables, over the meats. Serve with boiled potatoes.

Serves six to eight.

Blanquette of Goose

1 goose, 8 pounds (3½
    kg), cut into serving
    pieces
1 onion, stuck with 3 cloves
1 teaspoon dried thyme
1 sprig parsley
1 lemon slice

Salt and freshly ground
    black pepper
Cold water to cover
1 cup (¼ L) cream,
    blended with 2 egg
    yolks

Place the goose pieces in a kettle with the onion stuck with the cloves, the thyme, parsley, lemon slice, and salt and pepper to taste. Cover with boiling water, and simmer until tender, about 2 hours. Remove the goose to a hot platter or serving dish. Skim the fat off the broth and strain. Place 2 cups (½ L) broth in a saucepan and bring to a boil. Simmer for 5 minutes, taste for seasoning, and add the cream mixed with the egg yolks. Stir constantly until thickened (do not allow to boil) and pour over the goose. Serve with wild rice and buttered turnips.

Serves eight.

Poached Goose

1 goose, 8 to 10 pounds
    (3½–4½ kg)
Savory stuffing of your
    choice (see pages
    171–174)
Boiling water to cover
1 medium onion, finely
    chopped
Goose liver, chopped
¼ cup (60 g) rendered
    goose fat or bacon fat

Salt and freshly ground
    black pepper
1 cup (60 g) sliced mush-
    rooms
2 tablespoons chopped
    parsley
1 teaspoon dried tarragon
1 cup (¼ L) dry white wine
1 tablespoon (15 g) butter
1 tablespoon flour

Stuff the goose with a savory stuffing of your choice. Truss (see page 82), wrap securely in a heavily floured cloth, and tie. Place in a deep pot and cover with boiling water. Simmer for 1½ to 2 hours or more, until the goose is tender.

Sauté the onion and goose liver in the goose fat or bacon fat. Season with salt and pepper to taste and add the mushrooms, parsley, tarragon and white wine, and let simmer for 5 minutes. Add 1 cup (¼ L) of the degreased goose broth. Stir in a beurre manié (bits of the butter and flour blended together) till slightly thickened. Correct the seasoning.

Remove the goose from the kettle and unwrap. Serve on a large platter with the sauce, home-fried potatoes, and creamed turnips.

Serves 8.

New Year's Eve Goose in Aspic

1 goose, 8 to 10 pounds
(3½–4½ kg)
½ lemon
1 onion, stuck with 3 cloves
Bouquet garni (sprigs of
parsley, thyme, tarra-
gon, bay leaf, and
garlic, tied in cheese-
cloth)

1 cup (¼ L) wine vinegar
Salt and freshly ground
pepper
2 tablespoons (2 envelopes)
unflavored gelatin, dis-
solved in ¼ cup (½
dL) cold water
½ cup (1 dL) dry white
wine

Rub the goose well with half a lemon. Place the bird in a deep
pot with the onion stuck with the cloves, the bouquet garni, and
the wine vinegar. Cover with boiling water, and simmer till the
goose is tender, 1½ to 2 hours. Add salt and pepper to taste.

Remove the goose from the pot, allow it to cool, and skin it.
(The skin can be deep-fried, and the cracklings eaten as an
hors d'oeuvre.) Cut the bird into serving-sized pieces and remove the meat from the bones. Arrange in a large mold. Remove all the fat from the broth, reduce it by one-half, and
strain. Mix the dissolved gelatin with the white wine, and add
to the broth. Taste for seasoning and pour over the goose sections in the mold. Chill. Unmold on a large platter and serve
with mayonnaise and potato salad.

Serves eight.

Goose-Potato Skillet

4 tablespoons (60 g) rendered goose fat
1 medium onion, finely chopped
1 green pepper, seeded and finely chopped
1½ to 2 cups (170–225 g) finely diced roast goose

1½ pounds (680 g) potatoes, boiled, peeled, and diced
Salt and freshly ground black pepper to taste
1 package (10 ounces; 283 g) frozen chopped spinach, cooked and well drained
4 eggs
¼ cup (½ dL) milk

Heat the fat in a 10- to 12-inch (25–30 cm) skillet and sauté the onion and pepper gently until tender. Add the goose meat and potatoes and blend well. Add salt and pepper. Cover and cook over medium heat, stirring several times, for about 15 minutes, or until lightly browned. Loosely stir in the cooked spinach. Beat the eggs and the milk together and pour over the ingredients in the skillet. Cover and cook over low heat until firm. Serve cut into wedges.

Serves four.

Goose Hash

Leftover meat, carcass, and gravy from a roast goose
2 cups (½ L) water
2 medium onions, coarsely cut

3 tablespoons (45 g) rendered goose fat or butter
Any leftover stuffing
Salt and freshly ground black pepper

Cut the remnants of cold roast goose meat in small dice, and set aside. Put the carcass and leftover gravy in a pot, add the water, and simmer for 20 minutes.

Sauté the onions in the fat, then add any leftover stuffing, the goose meat, and salt and pepper to taste. Pour over this 1 cup (¼ L) of the cooking broth and let simmer, mixing frequently. Let cook down till rather dry. Serve with fried potatoes, cole slaw, and pickled beets or a beet and egg salad.

Goose Terrine with Filberts

½ pound (225 g) pork liver

½ pound (225 g) boneless pork shoulder

Breast from an uncooked goose, about ½ pound (225 g) after removing skin and bones

½ pound (225 g) slab bacon

2 eggs

2 tablespoons flour

1 cup (¼ L) dry white wine

½ cup (60 g) chopped shallots or sweet onion

½ cup (60 g) whole filberts, roasted and peeled

¼ pound (112 g) or more sliced bacon

Salt and freshly ground black pepper to taste

½ cup (1 dL) aspic (see below)

Using the metal blade in a food processor, coarsely chop the pork liver, pork shoulder, goose, and slab bacon; or use a meat grinder. Mix thoroughly with the eggs, flour, wine, shallots, filberts, and salt and pepper.

Line a terrine or ovenproof glass casserole with the bacon slices. Press in the ground mixture. Cover and refrigerate overnight. Next day, cover with a lid or foil, set in a pan of hot water, and bake in a preheated 350°F (175°C) oven for 2 hours. Uncover and drain off any excess fat. Pour ½ cup (1 dL) aspic over the top. Cool slightly, then refrigerate, covered, for 24 hours. Unmold on a serving plate and garnish as desired. Cut in slices to serve.

Serves eight.

ASPIC

1 can (10¾-ounce; 305 g) condensed beef bouillon

2 tablespoons Madeira or sherry

1 tablespoon (1 envelope) unflavored gelatin

2 tablespoons cold water

Soften the gelatin in the water. Heat all the ingredients together, stirring until the gelatin is dissolved.

Makes about 1½ cups (3½ dL).

Goose Rillettes

1 goose, 8 to 9 pounds
    (3½–4 kg), roasted
    and cooled, reserving
    some rendered fat
Salt
2 to 2½ pounds (900–
    1125 g) pork kidney
    fat or leaf lard

½ cup (1 dL) water
1 clove garlic
Freshly ground pepper
Dried thyme, to taste
    (optional)

Skin the goose, and cut the meat off the bones. Sprinkle the meat with salt and let stand for several hours. Combine with the pork fat or lard, the water, garlic, pepper and thyme (if you are using it) in a heavy casserole or braising pan. Add some of the rendered goose fat. Cook in a 300°F (150°C) oven for 4 hours or until the meat has cooked down thoroughly.

Pour into a colander set over a large pan to let the meat drain. When cool, shred the meat finely, using two forks. Pack in a crock, adding some of the fat as you go. Ladle fat over the top to completely seal. This will keep for several weeks under refrigeration. Serve like a pâté on bread or toast.

Liver-Goose Mold

2 tablespoons (30 g)
    rendered goose fat
1 pound (450 g) goose
    and chicken livers
Salt and freshly ground
    black pepper to taste
1 tablespoon (1 envelope)
    unflavored gelatin
1¼ cups (3 dL) goose
    broth (see page 122)

1 cup (115 g) finely diced
    roast goose
1 medium onion, chopped
½ cup (1 dL) cream
½ cup (1 dL) mayonnaise
    (page 181)
¼ teaspoon Worcestershire
    sauce

Heat the fat in a skillet, add the livers, and sauté until lightly browned, seasoning with salt and pepper to taste. Set aside. Sprinkle the gelatin over ¼ cup (½ dL) of the cold broth. Heat the remaining 1 cup (¼ L) broth and mix with the softened gelatin. In a food processor, smoothly blend the gelatin mixture, goose, onion, chicken livers, cream, and mayonnaise. (Or put the solid ingredients through a grinder, add the gelatin, cream, and mayonnaise, and blend until smooth.) Add the Worcestershire sauce and salt to taste.

Pour into a lightly oiled 1-quart (1 L) mold and chill until firm. Unmold on a serving plate and garnish as desired. Serve with crisp breads or crackers. This may also be served with greens as a main dish.

Liver Pâté with Mushrooms and Ham

3 tablespoons (45 g)
    rendered goose fat
1 cup (60 g) sliced
    mushrooms
½ pound (225 g) chicken
    livers
1 large goose liver,
    quartered
¼ cup (30 g) chopped
    onion

½ teaspoon salt
1 pound (450 g) minced
    ham
Optional garnishes:
    Chopped hard-boiled
    egg, chopped pis-
    tachios, finely sliced
    green onion

Heat the goose fat in a large skillet and sauté the mushrooms for 2 or 3 minutes. Add the chicken and goose livers, onion, and salt. Cover and simmer for 6 to 8 minutes, or just until the liver loses its pink color. Purée in a food processor or put through a meat grinder. Stir in the ham. Spread the mixture in an oiled 3-cup (¾ L) terrine or mold. Cover and refrigerate several hours or overnight. Unmold, top, if desired, with chopped hard-boiled egg, chopped pistachio nuts, or finely sliced green onion, and serve with cocktail rye bread or crackers.

Goose Giblets and Barley Soup

2 tablespoons (30 g)
    rendered goose fat
1 cup (115 g) sliced onion
Goose giblets and neck
4 cups (1 L) water
1 teaspoon salt

½ teaspoon celery salt
Any leftover roast goose
1 can (1 pound; 454 g)
    tomatoes, cut up
1 cup (170 g) pearl barley
½ teaspoon dried thyme

Heat the fat in a large, heavy pot and sauté the onion until limp but not brown. Add the giblets and neck, water, salt, and celery salt. Bring to a boil, then reduce the heat, cover, and simmer for 1 hour.

Remove the neck and giblets. Cut the meat off the neck and chop the giblets fine. Return to the kettle. If desired, add leftover cut-up roast goose. Add the tomatoes, barley, and thyme. Return to a boil, reduce heat, cover, and simmer 1 additional hour.

Serves six.

Cream of Goose Soup

2 leeks, cleaned and sliced
1 stalk celery, diced
4 tablespoons (60 g) butter
2 tablespoons flour
2 quarts (2 L) veal or
    chicken broth, or water

Carcass of 1 roast goose,
    plus neck and giblets
2 cups (½ L) heavy cream,
    blended with 3 egg
    yolks
Salt and freshly ground
    black pepper

Sauté the leeks and celery in the butter in a large, heavy pot until golden. Stir in the flour and brown lightly. Add the broth, goose carcass, neck, and giblets. Bring to a boil, then reduce heat, cover, and simmer about 2 hours. Strain and put the broth back in the pot. Add the cream mixed with the egg yolks. Heat, stirring constantly, until the soup is slightly thickened; do not allow to boil. Add salt and pepper to taste.

Serves six.

WILD GOOSE

Wild goose may be cooked in any way that you cook domestic goose. It is often very tough, however, and requires longer cooking.

6

Pheasant

Pheasant has a tendency to be dry and requires ample lubrication in cooking. Some sportsmen feel that it is not worth the shooting. But epicures generally favor the pheasant above most other game birds.

The battle over how long pheasant should be hung has waged on three continents for centuries. A smattering of English epicures still vow it is not fit to eat until decomposition has set in and a fetid odor is given off. I have seen pheasants in the markets of Europe so decomposed the bones had broken through and the flesh had discolored. Such birds, when cooked, have a distinct flavor that may best be described as "gamy." I prefer a pheasant that has hung about a week or 10 days, and I feel that a freshly killed bird has no distinguishing flavor.

Pheasants have been raised for shooting in England for generations. Great preserves dominated by a gamekeeper are filled with young pheasants every year and opened at the height of the season for the pleasure of the landowner and his guests. The pheasant was introduced into Europe centuries ago, in all probability from Asia, for the pheasant was originally named the Phasian bird, Phasis being a river in the ancient Asiatic province of Colchis.

In this country, pheasants are found wild in the upland states, sometimes in great profusion. Semiwild pheasants are raised in many parts of the country to supply restaurants and markets that specialize in game.

Definitely a luxury item, pheasant is worth having for any festive occasion.

Young pheasants are known by their short, rounded claws; old ones by their long and sharp ones.

Singe, draw, and clean pheasant as you do other game birds. Stuff with a savory stuffing or with celery, parsley, and onion, or just place a square of butter in each bird. One pheasant, generally 2½ to 3 pounds (1125–1350 g) in weight, will serve two or three people.

Roast Pheasant

Singe, clean, and stuff (if desired; see pages 169–175) a young pheasant. Bard it well with salt pork or bacon, being certain that the breast, which may be dry otherwise, is well covered. Place in a roasting pan with a small piece of butter and roast for 45 to 60 minutes in a 350° (175°C) oven. Baste every 10 minutes with drippings from the pan. When the bird is tender, remove to a hot platter.

Make a sauce in the roasting pan: Skim the excess fat from the pan and add 1 cup (¼ L) of broth made from simmering the chopped giblets in 1½ cups (3½ dL) salted water for 20 minutes. Blend well with the pan juices and add the chopped giblets and salt and pepper to taste. Thicken, if desired, with a beurre manié made of 1 tablespoon (15 g) butter blended with 1 tablespoon flour and added in bits. Stir till thickened. Serve with sautéed hominy squares. Or serve with the traditional English bread sauce that follows.

Serves two or three.

Bread Sauce

1 small onion, cut in small
   pieces
2 cups (½ L) milk
White bread crumbs,
   preferably dry

1 tablespoon (15 g) butter
Salt and freshly ground
   black pepper
2 tablespoons heavy cream

Simmer the onion pieces gently in the milk. When the milk seems sufficiently flavored, strain to remove the onion and add enough white bread crumbs to form a sauce the consistency of heavy cream. Add the butter as the mixture cooks—the cooking will

thicken it—and salt and pepper to taste. Finally stir in the heavy
cream.

Makes about 2½ cups (6dL).

Pheasant in Madeira

For this dish use a heavy metal pot deep enough to enclose the
bird under a tight cover.

1 young pheasant	8 tablespoons (115 g)
1 large onion	butter
1 stalk celery	¼ cup (½ dL) chicken
Salt and freshly ground	stock
black pepper to taste	1/3 cup (¾ dL) Madeira

Singe and clean the pheasant, then stuff with the onion and
celery and sprinkle with salt and pepper. Melt the butter in a
deep braising pan and brown the pheasant evenly. Regulate the
heat so that the butter browns but does not blacken. When the
bird is evenly browned—about 15 minutes—turn it breast side
down, clap the cover on tightly, and lower the heat. Cook, basting occasionally and turning. The bird should be done in 50 to 70
minutes in all, according to the size.

When done, remove to a hot platter and bring the pan juices
to boiling. Add the stock and taste for seasoning. Then add the
Madeira and bring just to boiling. Pass the sauce separately,
along with a bowl of crisp buttered bread crumbs.

Serves two.

Braised Pheasant with Yogurt

1 young pheasant	2 cups (½ L) yogurt
3 or 4 slices of bacon	3 teaspoons paprika
Salt and freshly ground	2 tablespoons chopped
black pepper	parsley

Preheat the oven to 450°F (230°C).

Singe, clean and stuff (if desired; see pages 169–175) the
pheasant. Bard it well with bacon, making certain the breast is
covered. Brown it in a heavy ovenproof casserole in the preheated oven for 20 minutes. Season with salt and pepper to taste
and add the yogurt, paprika, and chopped parsley. Cover, re-

duce the heat to 325°F (165°C) and cook for 25 minutes, or until tender. Serve with buttered noodles.

Serves two.

Braised Pheasant with Sauerkraut

2 pounds (900 g) sauer-
  kraut, drained
2 cups (½ L) chicken broth
1 cup (¼ L) white wine
Juniper berries

½ teaspoon caraway seeds
1 young pheasant
4 tablespoons (60 g)
  butter
Salt and pepper

Preheat the oven to 350°F (175°C).

Place sauerkraut in a deep earthenware or enameled iron casserole. Add the broth, white wine, a few juniper berries, and the caraway seeds. Cover and simmer for 1 hour in the oven.

Singe and clean the pheasant. Melt the butter in a skillet and brown the bird evenly on all sides. Season with salt and pepper to taste and place in the casserole with the sauerkraut. Cover and bake until the pheasant is tender, about 45 minutes to 1 hour. Serve on a hot platter surrounded with the sauerkraut.

Serves two.

Sautéed Pheasant with Cabbage

1 young pheasant
6 tablespoons (85 g) bacon
  fat or butter
1 medium head cabbage,
  finely shredded

Juniper berries (optional)
Salt and freshly ground
  black pepper
1 cup (¼ L) heavy cream
¼ teaspoon paprika

Singe, clean, and cut the pheasant in convenient serving pieces. Brown the pheasant in the bacon fat or butter in a large skillet. Reduce the heat, cover, and cook for 20 minutes.

Meanwhile, parboil the shredded cabbage in salted water for 10 minutes. Drain and season with salt to taste. Add the cabbage and a few juniper berries to the pheasant, cover the skillet, and allow it to cook for 10 minutes more. Add salt and pepper to taste and the cream, and simmer 5 minutes longer. Sprinkle with paprika and serve with boiled potatoes.

Serves two.

Sautéed Pheasant with Cream Gravy, Western Style

This is a typical western dish that I have enjoyed for many years and found to be one of the most delicious ways of eating pheasant. It has come down from the days when wild birds were one of the mainstays of families and were treated as everyday food rather than delicacies to be cherished and dressed up for company.

1 young pheasant
Flour
Salt and freshly ground
     black pepper

8 slices of bacon
2 cups (½ L) rich milk or
     half-and-half

Singe and clean the pheasant, then cut into convenient serving pieces. Dredge with flour, salt, and pepper. Fry the bacon in a heavy skillet till crisp. Remove the bacon slices to a hot plate, and quickly brown the pieces of pheasant on both sides in the hot fat. Season with salt and pepper to taste and reduce the heat. Cover the skillet and allow the pheasant to cook slowly for 20 minutes, turning once. Remove to a hot platter and dress with the crisp bacon. Skim off all but 3 tablespoons fat from the pan juices, add 3 tablespoons flour, and blend well over medium heat. Slowly add the milk, stirring constantly, and continue to stir till the mixture thickens. Season with salt and pepper to taste and serve in a gravy boat. Mashed potatoes and buttered cabbage are good with this dish. Add hot biscuits and honey and you have a delicious pioneer meal.

    Serves two.

Broiled Young Pheasant

Tender young pheasant may be split and broiled. The cooking
time should be from 15 to 18 minutes. It is essential to butter
the breasts well and baste frequently while broiling; otherwise
you get a dry bird. Season with salt and freshly ground black
pepper to taste and serve with fried hominy squares.

7

Quail

There are many varieties of quail abounding in the United States and in Europe, where they have been more popular than they ever were here. We have the bobwhite, which is prevalent in the eastern states; the crested or California quail; the valley quail; and the mountain quail. Some varieties are also called partridge. In parts of the country, domestic fresh quail are increasingly available, and I have become quite fond of serving these lovely morsels for a main course or as finger food for a cocktail party.

The English used to maintain that quail should not be drawn, and occasionally one finds an isolated case or two of the "eat the innards" school. To my knowledge, the only birds served with what is most descriptively and savagely called "the trail" are woodcock and snipe. I'll just take my birds empty or stuffed with something of my own making.

Quail should be quite fresh when cooked. The breasts need a covering of salt pork or bacon; for, like pheasant, the meat has a tendency to be dry. The roasting instructions I have given—I prefer a high temperature for small birds—should provide breast meat that is still moist and just slightly pink.

Gauge two quail per portion, unless very large, for a main course; and one, for a first course.

Whole Roast Quail

Singe and clean quail. Place a large lump of butter and a sprig of parsley in each one and wrap the breasts well with bacon. Place on a rack in a shallow pan and roast in a preheated 475°F

(245°C) oven, basting frequently in the bacon fat, for 20 minutes. Remove the bacon, and return the quail to the oven for another 3 to 4 minutes. Season with salt and pepper to taste. Add to the pan juices 1 cup (¼ L) broth, the poached and puréed livers of the birds, and salt and pepper to taste. Heat thoroughly. Serve the quail on buttered toast, and pass the sauce separately.

VARIATIONS

1. Stuff the birds with freshly opened oysters. Proceed as above and add a little of the oyster liquor to the sauce. Serve on toast with fried parsley.
2. Bard well, place a mushroom in each bird, wrap in cooking parchment and roast for 20 minutes in a 450°F (230°C) oven. Serve with sautéed mushrooms in cream.
3. Serve cold with a rémoulade sauce (see page 156) or homemade mayonnaise (see page 181).

Cicely Lucas's Quail on Scrapple

A recipe that is as thoroughly American as the Bucks County farmhouse from which it came.

6 quail
1 medium onion, chopped
Salt and freshly ground
        black pepper to taste
6 small onions

1 stalk celery, with leaves,
        cut in 6 pieces
6 strips bacon
1 cup (¼ L) good rich
        chicken stock
6 slices scrapple, sautéed

Preheat the oven to very hot (450°–500°F; 230°–260°C).

Singe and clean the birds, then rub with the chopped onion and salt and pepper. Stuff each bird with 1 small onion and a piece of celery with a bit of leaf as well. Lay a strip of bacon over each breast. Roast in the very hot oven, breast side up, for 5 minutes. Remove the bacon to absorbent paper. Turn the birds, breast down, add the chicken stock, and roast another 10 minutes, basting frequently. Finally turn the birds breast up once more and run under the broiler to brown, basting constantly. Do not overcook.

Remove the quail to a hot platter, arranging each bird on a

slice of cooked scrapple. Garnish with the bacon. Bring the pan juices to a boil, taste for seasoning, and serve in a sauceboat.
Serves three.

Split Roast Quail with Mustard I

6 quail, split down the back, well cleaned (reserve the giblets), and flattened
Dijon mustard
12 slices bacon
Salt and freshly ground black pepper
3 tablespoons (45 g) butter
Touch of Cognac
6 slices of buttered toast

Preheat the oven to 475°F (245°C).

Brush the quail breasts and legs of the quail with a fairly heavy coat of Dijon mustard, then tuck a slice of bacon over each half, covering legs, thighs, and breast section. Arrange the quail on the rack of the broiler pan, sprinkle lightly with salt and pepper, and roast in the preheated oven for 20 minutes; do not overcook. They need no basting because the bacon lubricates them. While the quail are roasting, sauté the giblets in butter until just cooked, seasoning them with salt, pepper, and a touch of Cognac, and chop them very fine.

Spread the buttered toast with a thin film of Dijon mustard and then with the sautéed, chopped giblets. Serve each quail on a piece of toast the minute they come from the oven and pour the juices left from sautéing over them.

Serve accompanied by a purée of carrots or turnip or some little Brussels sprouts, and drink a good dry white wine.

Serves three.

Split Roast Quail with Mustard II

8 to 10 quail, singed and cleaned
2 tablespoons Dijon mustard
2 tablespoons olive oil
16 to 20 slices bacon
Salt and freshly ground black pepper to taste

Preheat the oven to 475°F (245°C).

Split the quail and remove the wing tips. Brush with a blend of Dijon mustard and olive oil. Lay a strip of bacon around each half. Place on a rack in a small pan, skin side up, and roast in the preheated oven 20 minutes. Season with salt and pepper to taste. Serve as an entrée or as a cocktail hors d'oeuvre to be eaten with the fingers and with the aid of plenty of paper napkins.

Serves four to five as an entrée.

Broiled Quail

Singe, clean, and draw each quail, split down the back, and flatten. Rub well with butter or oil and place a goodly amount in the hollow of the rib cage. Broil for 8 to 10 minutes, turning several times and basting with butter. Season with salt and pepper to taste. Serve with braised celery.

Sautéed Quail with Madeira

2 quail
4 tablespoons (60 g)
    butter
Salt and freshly ground
    black pepper

¼ cup (½ dL) Madeira
2 tablespoons finely cut
    orange zest
2 slices buttered toast

Singe, clean, and split the quail down the back as for broiling. Melt the butter in a skillet and brown the quail very quickly on both sides over brisk heat. Reduce the heat and sauté gently for about 10 minutes. Season with salt and pepper to taste and add the Madeira and orange zest. Turn the quail well in this mixture. Serve on toast.

Serves one.

Sautéed Quail with Juniper Berries

9 tablespoons (130 g)
    butter
6 quail, cleaned, livers
    reserved
Salt and freshly ground
    black pepper

1 to 2 tablespoons chopped
    juniper berries
1 to 1½ cups (¼ L–
    3½ dL) water or
    broth, as needed
6 slices buttered toast

Melt 8 tablespoons (115 g) butter in a large skillet and brown the quail very quickly, turning the birds from side to side so they attain an evenness of color. Season with salt and pepper to taste and add the juniper berries. Cover, reduce the heat, and let them cook for 10 minutes.

Meanwhile, poach the quail livers till tender in salted water or broth to barely cover. Purée, add a tablespoon of butter, and keep warm. Serve the quail on buttered toast lightly spread with the liver purée, and pass the pan juices separately.

Serves three.

Sauté of Quail with White Grapes

6 slices stale bread about 2
    inches (5 cm) thick
6 quail, singed and cleaned
8 tablespoons (115 g)
    butter
Salt and freshly ground
    black pepper

½ cup (1 dL) chicken
    broth
6 tablespoons Cognac
1 cup (115 g) seedless
    white grapes

Make oval croustades of dry bread. They should be about 2 inches (5 cm) thick and just a bit larger than the quail. Hollow out a shallow cavity into which the quail will fit and toast the croustades gently in a slow oven. Butter the cavity into which you place the bird.

Brown the birds very quickly in butter. Season with salt and pepper to taste and add the broth. Cover, reduce the heat, and simmer for 10 minutes. Pour the Cognac over the birds and blaze them. Add the white grapes and shake the pan to coat them with the juices. Serve the quail and grapes in the croustades, and pass the pan juices separately.

Serves three.

Breast of Quail Sauté

Breast meat of 12 quail
8 tablespoons (115 g) butter
3 tablespoons chopped shallots

Salt and freshly ground black pepper
8 slices toast

Sauté the quail breasts in the butter for 5 to 6 minutes. Add the shallots and salt and pepper to taste. Cook briskly for another 2 minutes. Serve on toast.

Serves four.

Braised Stuffed Quail with White Wine

8 quail
2 teaspoons chopped shallots
11 tablespoons (155 g) butter
8 mushrooms, finely chopped
1 tablespoon chopped parsley
1 cup (115 g) dry bread crumbs

Salt and freshly ground black pepper
Fresh tarragon
Pinch of freshly grated nutmeg
½ cup (60 g) blanched, sliced almonds
1⅓ cups (3¼ dL) white wine
8 croustades or slices of toast

Preheat the oven to 375°F (190°C).

Singe and clean the quail. Make a stuffing by sautéing the chopped shallots in 3 tablespoons (45 g) butter. Add the mushrooms, chopped parsley, and bread crumbs, salt and pepper to taste, a few leaves of fresh tarragon, nutmeg, almonds, and 1/3 cup (¾ dL) white wine.

Stuff the quail. Melt 8 tablespoons (115 g) butter in an oven-proof skillet and brown the birds very quickly. Turn them breast side down and add 1 cup (¼ L) of white wine. Roast in the preheated oven for 15 minutes. Turn the birds breast side up and increase the heat to 450°F (230°C) for 3 to 4 minutes. Season with salt and pepper to taste and serve in croustades or on toast. Serve the pan juices separately.

Serves four.

8

Partridge

Many gallinaceous birds in this country are called partridge through ignorance or custom or for want of a better name. Hence, the bobwhite quail is called partridge in some locales. The bone structure and quality of flesh is similar in the two game birds, but there is a difference in plumage and coloring.

Wild partridge eaten before it has hung for 3 to 5 days is a rather dull and uninteresting dish. It needs the gamy quality to bring out the flavor. However, domestically raised partridge can be obtained fresh from game farms during most of the year—it will improve in flavor if hung for 5 or 6 days—and it is also sold frozen.

One partridge makes an adequate serving. Wild rice, mushrooms, cabbage, and carrots are all good accompaniments. In all honesty, I have seldom eaten tender partridge. It tends to be tough, and especially with wild partridge, one must look for young birds.

Roast Partridge

Singe and clean partridges. Rub well, inside and out, with lemon juice or half a lemon, and put a lump of butter in each cavity. Wrap salt pork or bacon around the breasts and secure with string. Push the legs toward the breasts, and secure them with a skewer pushed through the middle of the birds. Place on their sides on a rack in a roasting pan, and roast at 450°F (230°C) for 10 minutes, basting with butter. Turn to other side and roast for 10 minutes, again basting. Then remove the salt pork or bacon and turn breast side up for a final 10 minutes. Serve with bread sauce (page 136) or with the degreased pan juices mixed with the poached chopped giblets and salt and freshly ground black pepper to taste.

Allow 1 bird per person.

VARIATIONS

1. Serve with cabbage, prepared in this fashion: Place 1 shredded head of cabbage, 4 scraped, diced carrots, and a medium onion stuck with cloves in a kettle with ½ pound (225 g) pork, 6 bacon slices cut in strips, and 1 cup (¼ L) chicken broth. Cover and simmer for 1½ hours. Add ½ cup (1 dL) white wine after the first hour of cooking. Season with salt and freshly ground black pepper to taste. Arrange the roasted partridges on the cooked cabbage on a large hot platter. Serve with the degreased pan juices mixed with the poached, chopped giblets.
2. Serve with grilled, well-seasoned sausages and watercress.
3. Serve with grilled mushroom caps.

Broiled Partridge

Singe and clean young partridges, allowing 1 bird per portion. Split down the back and flatten. Rub well with butter. Place on a broiling rack in a preheated broiler and broil, skin side down, for 8 minutes. Season with salt and freshly ground black pepper to taste, then turn, baste with butter, and broil for another 7 or 8 minutes, till nicely browned and tender.

Meanwhile, poach the giblets till tender with an onion stuck with 2 cloves in 2 cups (½ L) water. Chop the giblets fine and mix with 1 tablespoon (15 g) butter and a little of the broth in which you cooked them. Spread slices of crisp well-buttered toast with this mixture and place half a partridge on a slice of toast. Pour over it the drippings from the pan and serve.

Broiled Deviled Partridge

Single and clean young partridges, then split down the back and flatten. Rub well with butter and place, skin side down, on a rack in a preheated broiler. Broil for 8 minutes. Turn, baste with butter, and broil for 5 minutes, or until nearly done. Remove and season with salt and pepper to taste. Brush well with buttter and then coat with toasted crumbs. Replace in the broiler for 2 or 3 minutes to brown slightly. Serve with deviled sauce (see below).

Deviled Sauce

½ cup (1 dL) white wine
2 tablespoons wine vinegar
1 bay leaf
6 peppercorns
1 small onion, stuck with 2
    cloves

2 tablespoons flour
2 tablespoons (30 g) butter
1 cup (¼ L) chicken broth
Salt and cayenne pepper to
    taste

Boil together the white wine, vinegar, bay leaf, peppercorns, and onion stuck with the cloves. When reduced to half, remove from the heat and strain. Blend the flour with the butter in a saucepan over medium heat, and let brown. Add the broth and stir well until thickened. Add the strained flavoring and blend well. Season with salt to taste and a generous sprinkling of cayenne.

Cold Partridge with Rémoulade Sauce

4 partridges
Giblets, poached in salted
    water and chopped
1 onion, finely chopped
2 tablespoons (30 g) butter
2 tablespoons chopped
    parsley

Juniper berries, crushed
1 cup (60 g) fresh bread
    crumbs
¼ cup (60 g) pine nuts
¼ cup (½ dL) sherry

Preheat the oven to 450°F (230°C).

Singe and clean the birds. Make a stuffing by sautéing the onion in the butter; then adding the poached, chopped giblets, parsley, a few crushed juniper berries, and the fresh bread crumbs. Mix well, remove from the heat, and add the pine nuts and sherry. Stuff the birds and secure them. Roast according to the preceding recipe; cool, but do not refrigerate.

Serve with rémoulade sauce or Cumberland sauce (see below) and green salad. This is an excellent supper or picnic dish. Serves four.

Rémoulade Sauce

1 ½ cups (3 ½ dL) mayon-
naise
1 tablespoon finely chopped
parsley
2 tablespoons finely
chopped capers

1 hard-boiled egg, finely
chopped
Lemon juice to taste
Salt and freshly ground
black pepper to taste

Blend all the ingredients well. For a more piquant flavor, omit the salt and add 2 or 3 finely chopped anchovies.

Makes about 2 cups (½ L).

Cumberland Sauce

Zest and juice of 1 orange
1 cup (¼ L) Madeira or
port
1 tablespoon lemon juice

½ cup (1 dL) currant jelly
Pinch of cayenne or ground
ginger

Cut the zest off the orange and chop it finely. Cook with the Madeira or port until the wine is reduced by one-third. Add the orange juice, lemon juice, currant jelly, and a small pinch of cayenne or ground ginger. Heat until the jelly is melted, and blend well. Serve cold.

Makes about 2 cups (½ L).

PRAIRIE HEN

This rather rare bird is restricted in its availability mostly to the West and Midwest. It may be prepared according to any of the recipes for partridge.

9

Snipe & Woodcock

SNIPE

Snipe are found in the coastal regions of the United States, but are comparatively little known in other parts of the country, hence they have never been as popular here as in England and France, where they are treasured. They are particularly popular with sportsmen for they are excellent shooting; their fast and irregular flight makes them a game bird almost without equal.

The snipe, which weighs from 2½ ounces to 8 ounces (70–225 g), has a long and functional beak which it uses for digging worms and bugs in bogs, swamps, and marshlands. The breast, truly the only worthwhile portion of the bird, is full and well-flavored. One snipe is a portion, though there are those who will eat more than that at a sitting.

Snipe are generally hung for 3 or 4 days. Like woodcock, they are seldom drawn. Those who are fond of eating them feel that the intestines and the giblets, called "the trail," give added flavor. They are sometimes drawn after they are cooked and the intestines chopped and mixed with the sauce in the pan. Traditionally they are cooked with the beak skewering the middle of the bird. The English favor bread sauce (page 136) or a dish of hot buttered crumbs served with the birds.

Broiled Snipe

Singe and clean the birds. Do not draw, but remove the gizzard. Rub well with butter and broil in a preheated broiler for 12 to

15 minutes. Baste well with butter or fat during broiling, and turn often so an evenness of color is assured on all sides. Serve on fried toast with bread sauce (page 136) or with a tart jelly and hominy squares, if you prefer. They are also delicious served on a crisp slice of scrapple.

Roast Snipe I

Singe and clean the birds. Do not draw, but remove the gizzard. Cover the breasts with salt pork or bacon and place in a buttered baking dish. Place in a 475°F (245°C) oven and roast for 20 minutes. Season with salt and pepper to taste. Serve with the pan juices.

VARIATIONS

1. When the snipe are cooked, remove the intestines and cut them into fine pieces. Sauté them in the fat from the baking dish and season to taste. Add ¼ cup (½ dL) Cognac and mix well. Pour the sauce over the birds on a heated platter and add another ¼ cup (½ dL) Cognac. Flambé and serve.
2. Follow the first variation, but add 1 tablespoon minced shallots to the sauce. Cut the birds in half and bathe them well in the sauce. Flambé.
3. Add ½ cup (1 dL) Madeira to the pan juices. Heat and serve.
4. Baste the snipe with a little orange juice during cooking and add finely cut shreds of orange zest and ½ cup (1 dL) Madeira to the sauce.

Roast Snipe II

Singe, draw and clean the snipe. Put 2 or 3 juniper berries in the cavity, brush the skin with oil, and season with salt and pepper. Roast on a rack for 20 minutes in a 475°F (245°C) oven, basting two or three times with oil or butter. Remove from the oven, and flame with gin. Serve on fried toast.

Salmi of Snipe

Snipe, singed and cleaned,
    giblets reserved if
    desired
6 to 7 tablespoons (85–
    100 g) butter
2 tablespoons finely
    chopped shallots
1 clove garlic, finely
    chopped

1 cup (¼ L) chicken broth
Salt and freshly ground
    black pepper
3 tablespoons flour
½ cup (1 dL) Madeira or
    sherry
Juniper berries
Pinch of ground cloves
Pinch of ground ginger

Roast or broil snipe as directed on pages 159–161, then season and serve with the following sauce: Heat 3 tablespoons (45 g) butter in a skillet. Add the shallots and garlic and sauté till transparent. Add the broth and simmer for 5 minutes. Strain, and season with salt and pepper to taste. In a saucepan over medium heat, blend an additional 3 tablespoons (45 g) butter and the flour. Gradually stir in the strained broth and Madeira or sherry, and stir till properly thickened. Add a few juniper berries and the cloves and ginger.

Let the birds cook in this sauce for 5 or 6 minutes, adding the pan juices. You may also add the chopped giblets, sautéed in 1 tablespoon (15 g) of butter.

WOODCOCK

Woodcock is a small game bird, related to the snipe, that is much relished in England and France. Although they are not easy to come by in the United States, I have eaten them in New

York and in the South. They are a nuisance to pick if you get them in feather but are well worth the trouble. After cleaning them, wrap in a damp towel, and store in the refrigerator for 4 or 5 days to mature in flavor. They can be prepared according to any of the recipes given for snipe.

10

Dove

Dove has always had a great public in the South. It is a fine target for the hunter and a rewarding dish for the food fancier. Oftentimes, however, it is overcooked, to become a rather unappetizing dish—the fault of recipes inherited from the past. This delicate bird requires very little elaboration; it is best when cooked simply.

Barbecued or Broiled Doves

6 doves
½ lemon
1 cup (115 g) finely
    chopped tart apple
¾ cup (85 g) finely
    chopped onion
1 teaspoon salt
Freshly ground black pepper

¼ teaspoon freshly grated
    nutmeg
¼ cup (½ dL) melted
    butter
12 slices bacon
½ cup (1 dL) medium-dry
    sherry or Madeira

Singe and clean the doves, then rub the cavities well with the half a lemon. Combine the apple, onion, seasonings and butter, and spoon into the birds. Wrap 2 slices of bacon around each and place on a broiling rack. Grill over medium coals, or about 6 inches (15 cm) from the broiling unit. Turn them often till nicely colored. Transfer to a rack in a roasting pan or heated casserole. Add the sherry or Madeira, cover, and braise in a 250°F (120°C) oven for 10 minutes. Pour the pan juices over the birds. Serve with corn pudding or spoon bread and a salad.
    Serves six.

Braised Dove

This is a delightful way to treat small game birds, and really no trouble.

2 slices bacon, cut in small pieces
1 shallot, very finely chopped
2½ tablespoons chopped parsley
4 small white onions
Dried thyme
3 tablespoons (45 g) butter
2 doves, cleaned and drawn

Pinch of dried sweet basil
Pinch of dried chervil
2/3 cup (1½ dL) chicken broth
1 tablespoon glace de viande (concentrated beef glaze)
½ cup (115 g) pitted green olives

Preheat the oven to 450°F (230°C).

Cook the bacon very gently in a flameproof baking dish with the chopped shallot and 1½ tablespoons chopped parsley. Add the onions and a pinch of thyme, toss to blend, and allow the onions to brown very slightly. Pour off the bacon fat and remove bacon bits to a warm dish. Heat 1 tablespoon (15 g) butter in the baking dish, and sear the birds very quickly.

Mix the remaining butter with a pinch of thyme, sweet basil, chervil, and another tablespoon of parsley. Divide in half and insert in the cavity of each bird. Pour the chicken broth over them. Place in a hot 450°F (230°C) oven, and bake for 12 minutes. If the broth cooks down too quickly, add more.

Finally, add the glace de viande to the pan juices, along with the bacon bits and olives. Cook up very quickly, correct the seasoning, and remove the birds to a warm platter. Skim off the excess fat from the sauce, and serve with the birds.

Serves two.

11

Stuffings

Basic Bread Stuffing

FOR TURKEY

One of the simplest and best stuffings is prepared the following way. Gauge about ¾ to 1 cup of stuffing per pound (450 g) of turkey.

2 large onions, finely chopped

10 tablespoons (145 g) butter

9 cups (510 g) stale bread crumbs or toasted crumbs

2½ cups (285 g) finely cut celery

2½ teaspoons dried thyme and marjoram, mixed

2½ tablespoons chopped parsley

Salt and freshly ground black pepper

Sauté the onion in 2½ tablespoons (35 g) butter till transparent. Add the remaining butter, allow to melt, and blend with the crumbs and seasonings.

Makes about 12 to 13 cups.

VARIATIONS

1. Add ⅓ cup (35 g) chopped green pepper or pimiento.
2. Add 2½ cups (140 g) sliced mushrooms, sautéed in 8 tablespoons (115 g) butter.
3. Add 1¼ cups (140 g) diced smoked ham, sautéed in a little fat.
4. Add 1¼ cups (140 g) crisply fried bacon slivers.
5. Add 1¼ cups (140 g) blanched almonds.

6. Add 1¼ cups (140 g) salted peanuts.
7. Add 1¼ cups (140 g) coarsely chopped tart apple.
8. Add the chopped giblets of the bird, sautéed in butter.
9. Substitute cornbread for the bread crumbs.
10. Add 2½ cups (565 g) sausage meat, browned quickly in the skillet.
11. Add 1¼ cups (140 g) raisins, soaked in sherry.

Tarragon Crumb Stuffing

FOR TURKEY

2 cups (225 g) finely chopped scallions or shallots
¾ pound (340 g) butter
10 cups (565 g) fresh bread crumbs, preferably from French or Italian bread, part whole-wheat if desired

1 tablespoon or more dried tarragon
½ cup (30 g) chopped parsley
2 teaspoons salt, or to taste
1 teaspoon freshly ground black pepper
Sherry, Cognac, or turkey broth, if needed

Place the scallions or shallots in a skillet with the butter, and heat until the butter is melted. Blend with the crumbs, herbs, and seasonings and toss well. Taste for salt. If the stuffing is too dry, moisten with a bit of sherry, Cognac, or turkey broth.

Makes about 14 cups.

Sausage Stuffing

FOR TURKEY

2 pounds (900 g) good sausage meat
1½ teaspoons salt
1 teaspoon dried thyme
1 teaspoon Tabasco
1 teaspoon ground coriander

1 teaspoon freshly ground black pepper
1 pound (450 g) ground veal or ham
¾ cup (85 g) pine nuts
½ cup (30 g) finely chopped parsley

Blend all ingredients together thoroughly. Test for seasoning by sautéing about 2 teaspoons in butter.

Makes about 7 or 8 cups.

Brazil Nut Stuffing

FOR TURKEY

3 cups (170 g) bread
  crumbs, toasted
1 cup (225 g) ground fresh
  pork without fat
4 tablespoons (60 g) butter
4 large white onions, finely
  chopped
½ cup (30 g) sliced mush-
  rooms

½ cup (60 g) chopped
  celery
½ teaspoon dried thyme
½ teaspoon dried rosemary
Salt and freshly ground
  black pepper to taste
1 cup (115 g) Brazil nuts
½ cup (1 dL) sherry, or as
  needed

Mix the bread crumbs with the pork. Heat the butter in a large
skillet and sauté the chopped onion till transparent. Add the
mushrooms, celery, and herbs. Blend well over low heat. Add
to the crumb and pork mixture and season well with salt and
pepper. If you want to taste for salt, sauté a small amount; do
not eat raw.

Blanch the Brazil nuts by immersing them in boiling water.
Slip the skins off with fingers or a dull knife. Add them to the
mixture, along with enough sherry to moisten thoroughly.

Makes 8 to 9 cups.

Potato Stuffing

FOR GOOSE OR TURKEY

4 tart apples, cored, peeled,
  and quartered
4 medium onions, chopped
2 cups (½ L) broth (made
  from the neck and
  giblets simmered in
  water)

1 sprig parsley
½ teaspoon dried thyme
½ teaspoon dried rosemary
3 cups (675 g) hot riced
  potatoes
2 tablespoons (30 g) butter

Simmer the apples and onion in the broth till tender. Add the
parsley, thyme, and rosemary. Force through a fine sieve and
mix with the hot riced potatoes. Add the butter and whip until
fluffy.

Makes about 10 cups.

Chestnut Stuffing

FOR DUCK, GOOSE, OR TURKEY

1 pound (450 g) unshelled
    chestnuts
1 large onion, finely
    chopped
8 tablespoons (115 g)
    butter
2 tablespoons chopped
    parsley
½ teaspoon dried thyme

½ teaspoon dried rosemary
Salt and freshly ground
    black pepper
3 cups (340 g) dry bread
    crumbs
Giblets, chopped and
    sautéed in butter (op-
    tional)

Slit the skin crosswise on the flat side of each chestnut, and roast
or boil the chestnuts till tender. (Roasting them is my preference.) Shell and skin them and break into bits.

Sauté the onion in 4 tablespoons (60 g) butter till transparent. Add the herbs. Blend with the dry bread crumbs and
chestnuts, and salt and pepper to taste. Lubricate with the remaining butter, melted. Add chopped sautéed giblets if you like.

Makes 7 to 8 cups.

Oyster Stuffing

FOR TURKEY

1 large onion, finely
    chopped
2 tablespoons chopped
    green pepper
3 tablespoons (45 g) butter
    or rendered fat from
    the bird
¼ pound (115 g) bacon,
    cut in tiny slivers

3 cups (340 g) dry bread
    crumbs
Salt and freshly ground
    black pepper
½ teaspoon dried thyme
1 quart (1 kg) raw oysters,
    chopped
½ cup (1 dL) oyster liquor

Sauté the onion and green pepper in the butter or rendered fat.
In another skillet, try out the bacon slivers until crisp. Add the
bacon, onion, and green pepper to the dry bread crumbs and
season to taste. Add the chopped oysters and oyster liquor and
mix well.

Makes about 10 cups.

Rice Giblet Stuffing

FOR TURKEY

1½ cups (255 g) raw rice
Giblets, very finely chopped
1 large onion, very finely
    chopped
1 clove garlic, very finely
    chopped
4 tablespoons (60 g) butter
½ cup (30 g) chopped
    parsley

½ teaspoon dried thyme
½ teaspoon dried rosemary
½ teaspoon dried marjoram
Pinch of ground ginger
Salt and freshly ground
    black pepper
½ cup (60 g) broken
    walnut meats

Cook the rice in boiling, salted water till fluffy and tender.

Sauté the giblets, onion, and garlic in the butter until delicately browned. Add to the rice, along with the parsley, thyme, rosemary, marjoram, ginger, and salt and pepper to taste. Last, add the walnut meats and mix well.

Makes about 7 cups.

Simple Apple Stuffing

FOR WILD DUCK

Equal quantities of chopped apple, onion, and celery mixed with a little rosemary and marjoram and lightly dusted with mace and nutmeg make a superb stuffing for duck or almost any wild game bird.

Nutted Ham Stuffing

FOR CAPON, CHICKEN OR A SMALL TURKEY

1 medium onion, finely
    chopped
3 tablespoons (45 g) butter
½ pound (225 g) smoked
    ham, ground
1 cup (115 g) chopped
    celery

1½ cups (85 g) fresh
    bread crumbs
½ cup (115 g) pine nuts
½ cup (1 dL) sherry
½ teaspoon dried rosemary
Salt and freshly ground
    black pepper

Sauté the onion in butter. Mix with ham and the other ingredients and season to taste.

Makes about 5 cups

Sauerkraut Stuffing

FOR DUCK OR GOOSE

In many European countries, sauerkraut has long been a traditional stuffing for duck and goose, as well as pheasant and turkey. It provides a delicious complementary flavor.

1 large onion, thinly sliced
¼ cup (60 g) butter or
    other fat
1 pound (450 g) sauerkraut

1 teaspoon caraway seeds
1 tart apple, finely chopped
1 cup (¼ L) white wine

Sauté the onion in the butter or other fat. When nicely browned, add the sauerkraut, caraway seeds, and apple. Toss well in the pan for 5 minutes, then add the white wine and simmer for 5 minutes more.

Makes 6 to 7 cups.

Apple and Chestnut Stuffing

FOR GOOSE

Pare, core and halve 4 to 12 apples, according to the size of your bird. Slit the skins of 1 to 2 pounds (450–900 g) of chestnuts. Boil till tender and skin them. Sprinkle with salt and freshly grated nutmeg. Alternate the apples and chestnuts inside the bird and pack very tightly. Sew up the vent and roast. The apples and chestnuts will blend into a most delectable stuffing. A few prunes soaked in white wine for 6 hours may be added, if desired.

Sweet Potato and Mincemeat Stuffing

FOR DUCK, GOOSE OR TURKEY

4 cups (900 g) mashed and
    buttered sweet potatoes
1 cup (115 g) coarsely
    chopped tart apples

2 cups (450 g) mincemeat
½ cup (1 dL) brandy
½ teaspoon mace
½ teaspoon ground ginger

Blend the sweet potatoes with the tart apples, and mix in the mincemeat flavored with the brandy, mace, and ginger.

Makes about 7 cups.

Matzoh Stuffing

FOR CHICKEN OR TURKEY

3 tablespoons (45 g) butter
  or rendered fat from
  the bird
Giblets, chopped
2 onions, finely chopped
Salt and freshly ground
  black pepper
5 to 8 matzohs or dry water
  biscuits

4 egg yolks, beaten
¼ teaspoon dried thyme
¼ teaspoon dried marjoram
Pinch of freshly grated
  nutmeg
1 tablespoon grated fresh
  ginger

Sauté the chopped giblets and onions in the butter or rendered fat from the bird. Season with salt and pepper to taste. Transfer the giblets and onion to a dish.

Soak matzohs or dry water biscuits in water. Drain, squeeze dry, and add to the fat in the pan in which you sautéed the giblets. Stir well over a very low flame and add to the giblets. Add the egg yolks, herbs, and spices. Blend well and correct the seasoning.

Makes about 4 cups.

12

Basic Sauces

Béchamel Sauce (Basic White Sauce)

2 tablespoons (30 g) butter
2 tablespoons flour
1 cup (¼ L) milk, broth,
    or other liquid, heated

Salt and freshly ground
    black pepper
Freshly grated nutmeg

Melt the butter in a heavy saucepan over low heat and stir in the flour. Blend well for 2 or 3 minutes and gradually add the hot milk or broth. Increase the heat slightly and stir until the mixture is smooth and thickened. Allow to simmer for 3 or 4 minutes more. Season with salt and pepper to taste, and add a few grains of nutmeg.

    Makes 1 cup (¼ L) of sauce.

Note: For a thick white sauce, use 1 tablespoon more of butter and flour.

VARIATIONS

Velouté Sauce: Add ½ cup (1 dL) heavy cream to the béchamel sauce (see above), simmer for a few minutes, and then beat in 3 tablespoons (45 g) butter, one at a time.

Sauce Suprême: Use rich chicken broth for the liquid in making the béchamel sauce (see above). Combine 3 lightly beaten egg yolks with 1 cup (¼ L) heavy cream. Stir in a little of the sauce to warm the eggs, and then stir this mixture back into the sauce. Simmer over low heat, but do not allow to boil.

Mornay Sauce: To the béchamel sauce (see above), add ¼ to ½ cup (20–45 g) freshly grated Parmesan cheese and blend thoroughly.

Cheese Sauce: Add ½ cup (45 g) grated sharp Cheddar or Swiss cheese to the béchamel sauce (see above), and heat just until the cheese melts.

Hollandaise Sauce

HAND METHOD

3 or 4 egg yolks
½ teaspoon salt
1 tablespoon lemon juice
Dash of Tabasco

8 tablespoons (115 g) butter, cut into small pieces
1 tablespoon hot or cold water, if needed

Place a small, heavy saucepan (enameled cast iron preferred) over low heat or the top of a double boiler over hot, not boiling, water. Put 3 egg yolks, the salt, 1 tablespoon lemon juice, and Tabasco in the pan and beat with a wire whisk or electric hand mixer until well blended and the eggs have slightly thickened. Have the butter ready on a warm plate. Start adding the butter, beating in a piece at a time until it is absorbed. Do not add too quickly. Continue to beat until the sauce is thick. If it is too thick, add a tablespoon of cold water.

BLENDER METHOD

Use the ingredients given above, with 1 tablespoon lemon juice and adding the extra egg yolk. Combine all the ingredients except the butter and water in the blender container. Turn on and off at high speed just long enough to blend. Heat the butter in a saucepan until it is hot and foaming, but do not allow it to brown. Turn the blender to high speed, and very slowly and steadily pour in the butter. If the sauce curdles, add 1 tablespoon hot water while blending.

FOOD PROCESSOR METHOD

Use the ingredients given above, adding the extra egg yolk and an extra tablespoon of lemon juice. Process all the ingredients, except the butter and water, for a few seconds, using the metal blade. Then continue to process while you gradually pour in hot, foaming (not browned) butter.

Makes about 1 cup.

Sauce Béarnaise

1 tablespoon finely chopped
    shallots or scallions
1 tablespoon chopped fresh
    tarragon, more if de-
    sired, or 1 teaspoon
    dried

¼ cup (½ dL) wine
    vinegar
¼ cup (½ dL) white wine
1 teaspoon chopped parsley
Hollandaise sauce (see page
    180)

Combine the shallots or scallions, tarragon, wine vinegar, white wine, and chopped parsley. Bring to a boil and reduce to practically a glaze, about 2 tablespoons. Add this to the hollandaise sauce, just before you add the butter. If tarragon is fresh, it is sometimes pleasant to stir an extra amount into the finished sauce.

Homemade Mayonnaise

HAND METHOD
2 egg yolks
1 teaspoon salt
½ teaspoon dry mustard
1½ cups (3½ dL) good
    olive oil, or a mixture
    of olive oil and
    vegetable oil

1 tablespoon lemon juice or
    white wine vinegar

Put the egg yolks, salt, and mustard in a bowl and beat with a wire whisk or hand beater till the yolks have thickened. Begin to add the oil a few drops at a time, beating after each addition, until the mixture begins to emulsify and thicken, at which point the oil can be added in tablespoons. After all the oil has been incorporated, beat in the lemon juice or vinegar. This will keep 1 week under refrigeration.

Note: If the emulsion separates, start over with 1 egg yolk in a clean bowl, beating in a bit of oil and then the original mixture.

Makes 1¾ cups (4 dL).

BLENDER METHOD

2 whole eggs
1 teaspoon salt
½ teaspoon dry mustard
1 tablespoon lemon juice or
    white wine vinegar

1 ½ cups olive oil, or a mix-
    ture of olive oil and
    vegetable oil

Put the eggs, salt, mustard, and lemon juice or vinegar in the container of the blender, and run at high speed for about 5 seconds. Remove the cover insert, turn on the blender, and pour in the oil in a very thin, steady stream. Blend until the emulsion is smooth and then turn off at once.

Makes about 2 cups (½ L).

FOOD PROCESSOR METHOD

1 whole egg
1 tablespoon white wine
    vinegar
½ teaspoon dry mustard

½ teaspoon salt
¼ teaspoon freshly ground
    white pepper
1 cup (¼ L) olive oil

Put the egg, vinegar, mustard, salt, and pepper in the beaker of the food processor, fitted with the metal blade. Process about 2 to 3 seconds, or until blended; then, very slowly at first, pour the oil through feed tube until it has all been incorporated and the emulsion has thickened. Taste for seasoning.

Makes about 1 ¼ cups (3 dL).

Note: If the mayonnaise should separate, put 2 egg yolks in a clean beaker, start to process, and gradually pour in the original mixture.

Index

Filberts, goose terrine with, 129
Fowl
  in Creole chicken, 31
  notes on, xi, 4
  in poached chicken farm style, 28
Fricassees. *See* Chicken
Fried chicken. *See* Chicken

Game bird. *See* Cornish game hen
Garlic, forty cloves of, chicken with, 54
Giblet(s)
  basic bread stuffing with, 170
  chopped, sandwich, 72
  goose, and barley soup, 131
  rice, stuffing (for turkey), 173
  sauce for roast chicken, 39
  sauté, 72
Golden State goose, 124
Goose
  Alsatian style, 125
  blanquette of, 125
  broth, 122
  cream of, soup, 132
  frozen, to thaw, 121
  giblets and barley soup, 131
  Golden State, 124
  gravy, 123
  hash, 128
  liver, in liver pâté with mushrooms and ham, 131
  liver-, mold, 130
  New Year's Eve, in aspic, 127
  notes on, 121–22
  poached, 126
  -potato skillet, 128
  rillettes, 130
  roast, 122
    in a microwave oven, 122
    sauce for, 123
  soup, cream of goose, 132
  stuffings for, 171–72, 174
  terrine with filberts, 129
  wild, notes on, 132
Grapes, white
  sauté of quail with, 147

Grapes, white (*cont.*)
  seedless, in traditional chicken salad, 66
Gravy
  browned, Virginia fried chicken with, 20
  cream, sautéed pheasant with, western style, 139
  goose, 123
Green beans, in traditional chicken salad, 65
Green pepper, basic bread stuffing with, 169
Grilled leftover turkey legs, 92
Grouse, domestic, unavailability of, xiii

Ham
  basic bread stuffing with, 169
  in composed sandwich, 67
  liver pâté with mushrooms and, 131
  a (chicken) sauté with, 11
  stuffing, nutted (for capon, chicken, or a small turkey), 173
  turkey and, in aspic, 93
Hash
  chicken. *See* Chicken
  goose, 128
  turkey, 92
    smoked turkey for, 95
Hen
  prairie, notes on, 157
  see also Fowl
Herbed butter, roast chicken with, 38
Herbs
  a (chicken) sauté with white wine and
    I, 6
    II, 7
  squab sauté with white wine and, 114
Hollandaise sauce, 180
Homemade mayonnaise, 181

Turkey (*cont.*)
  tonnato, 93
  truffled, 83
  wild
    availability of, xii
    North American, to roast, 95
  wings
    braised, 87
    braised, chili, 87
    braised, provençal, 87
    braised, with white wine and
      tarragon, 87
    teriyaki, 84
    uses for, xi

Velouté sauce, 179
Viennese (chicken) sauté, a, 12
Virginia fried chicken with browned
  gravy, 20

Walnuts, English, in traditional
  chicken salad, 66
Watercress, roast partridge with
  sausages and, 154
Whole roast quail, 143

Wild duck. *See* Duck, wild
Wild goose, notes on, 132
Wild rice, turkey and, casserole, 89
Wild turkey. *See* Turkey, wild
Wine, white
  braised stuffed quail with, 148
  casserole of chicken with, 52
  fricassee of chicken with, 47
  and herbs
    a (chicken) sauté with, I, 6
    a (chicken) sauté with, II, 7
    squab sauté with, 114
  and tarragon, braised turkey
    wings with, 87
Woodcock
  notes on, 161–62
  see also Snipe
Wood pigeon, casserole of, with
  sauerkraut, 117

Yogurt
  braised pheasant with, 137
  casserole of duck with, 102
  squab sauté with cabbage and,
    115